Lick the Spoon!

GW 1.99

Mairlyn Smith's Favourite Recipes

Macmillan Canada
Toronto

Canadian Cataloguing in Publication Data

Smith, Mairlyn
   Lick the spoon : Mairlyn Smith's favourite recipes

Includes index.
ISBN 0-7715-7561-0

1. Cookery. I. Title.

TX714.S64 1998   641.5   C97-932193-X

This book is available at special discounts for bulk purchases by your group or organization for sales promotions, premiums, fundraising and seminars. For details, contact: Macmillan Canada, Special Sales Department, 29 Birch Avenue, Toronto, ON M4V 1E2. Tel: 416-963-8830.

Cover and interior design: David Vereschagin
Cover photo: Karen Wylie/Coyote Photos
Hair and makeup: Diane Mazur

Macmillan Canada
A Division of Canada Publishing Corporation
Toronto, Ontario, Canada

1 2 3 4 5 TRI 02 01 00 99 98

Printed in Canada

To my mom,
who let me cook anything I wanted to;
to my dad for eating it;
and to my son,
who tried most of Mommy's experiments.

Acknowledgement

One day way back in 1993, I was watching "Oprah" (my son was still taking his blessed naps!). Her show that day was about goals. She gave a list of questions that helped her focus her life. Here they are:

What do I want to be?
What do I want to do?
What do I want to have?
What do I want to give?

I watched that whole show, got right off my big old derrière, and answered all those questions. Suddenly on paper the goals in my life looked me right in the eye. Some were big; some, small. Some were doable in one month; some, in five years. Some it would take my whole life to accomplish.

Oprah Winfrey's show always affects me in some way, but that day my life changed.

I'd like to thank Oprah for inspiring me. I learned that the only thing that was holding me back from getting on with my life was that first step. Here's to the many steps it's taken me to get here.

All books and lives need people to thank. Here is my list.

Mom and Dad, who really are the main reason I started cooking. Special thanks for eating 36 years of experiments.

Andrew, for being patient while Mommy cooked her experiments.

Scott Wickware, the biggest taster ever. I know he enjoyed being on the "meal plan," and he didn't even complain when he gained weight. He is my "world-famous" taster.

My sister, Kathleen Fairweather, who couldn't believe she liked healthy stuff.

My brother, John Smith, who washed the dishes after I baked when I was a kid. I loved making big messes!

Nina Roberts, who listened to me whine and made me laugh.

Michale Brode, for years of laughter and friendship, and for being the only person I can cook with.

Jann Stefoff, who has always encouraged and supported me.

Joanne Sigal, who continues to keep me normal and is one of the best cooks I know.

Marianne McIsaac, for proofing the recipes and eating all the experimental Chocolate Caramel Pecan Cheesecakes.

Evelyne Carter, who said "yea" or "nay."

Jane Giffen, who makes me laugh and is the best food stylist in town.

Anne Pick, Janice Dawes, and Susan Fleming from Stone Soup Productions, for giving me a big break and hiring me for "Harrowsmith."

Anne Pick, again, for letting me say all the things I want to say on the show.

Karen O'Reilly, who first showed interest in this book.

Alison Maclean at Macmillan, who picked up the ball and offered me this book.

Gerry Lomberg, my agent — who thinks I'm funny.

Donna Trimble, my agent — who thinks I'm funny, sometimes.

Bryan Misener at Characters, who happens to be the only person who can leave me speechless.

The staff at Gledhill P.S., for tasting treats.

Lesley Grant of Word Nerd, for inputting all the longhand—she was very patient.

Nicole de Montbrun, who has "talked me down" a couple of times already—"Don't jump, Mair, it'll be fine." She's so calm!

The crew of "Harrowsmith Country Life": Wally Corbett, for lighting me better than the fridge; Bruce Cameron, for making sure the mike is working on my upper torso; Rick Boston, for laughing at my awful jokes; John Kajfes, who can find wherever I am in the script; Diane Mazur, who does my hair and make-up; Alex Newman, for mincing onions; and Jane Giffen, again, for being a fabulous food stylist.

And finally, all of Scott's and my friends who ate everything I've cooked in the past couple of years!

Thank you.

Contents

Introduction

I love to eat. I really like tasting things and trying to figure out what's in them. I always thought this guessing game would make a great game show. I'd call it "What Am I Chewing?" The three contestants would eat something—say, chocolate mousse cake—and they'd have to list the ingredients. The first one with all the right ingredients would win the cake. Okay, it's a low-budget Canadian game show—in the States, the winner would take home a car!

I started cooking when I was four. My mom let me help bake brownies. One lick of the spoon and I was hooked for life.

Cooking is my creative hobby. Some people make quilts, others do needlepoint, some paint. Me—I get to eat my hobby. Hey, there's an interesting concept—you get to eat what you make. I bet the needlepoint class wouldn't be crowded if that was their slogan.

Cooking offers instant results. I can try out a recipe and decide within a couple of hours whether or not it is good. Sewing? I have to wait a whole week to see if I look good in that dress. And usually the experience is very anticlimactic. The dress looks awful. I guess when it comes right down to it, I just really love to cook.

On "Harrowsmith Country Life" one of my goals is to demystify cooking because I believe if you can read, you can cook. You just need to be reading the right thing. I've included a glossary and a list of techniques and methods, so if you come across a new word, look it up. Read it and then do it.

Cooking should also be fun. Well, for that matter, so should life. If it's not, you have the power to change it.

There is only one thing that bugs me about cooking: it's the fact that it may take two-and-a-half hours to prepare an especially nice dinner, which is eaten in five-and-a-half minutes. I feel that out of respect for the cook there should be an International Standard of Eating Time. Basically, the formula would be as follows: every 30 minutes of preparation requires 15 minutes of eating. So a one-hour prep would result in 30 minutes of eating. Instead of telling everyone how long you slaved over the meal, tell them they have 45 minutes to eat it. This puts a whole new spin on Thanksgiving. After three hours of eating, you'd be thankful you didn't have to sit by weird Auntie Sara every night.

I had so much fun writing this book; mind you, I haven't been in hysterics about the 11 pounds I gained in the process. On second thought, hysterical is probably close to how I acted when I finally got the nerve to stand on the scale. I think my next book better be about low-fat cooking.

I wanted this book to teach as much as entertain. My apologies to the experienced cooks who feel I'm overexplaining. The rest of you—I hope the details help make the finished product easy to make.

It took me nine months to write this book. I did it in longhand on the backs of film or television scripts. I've got to get into the nineties and buy a computer.

The day after I tested my last recipe, I went out for lunch with my friend Jann to our regular lunch place, the Olympus, and I ordered french fries, a chocolate milkshake, and pickles. They asked if I was pregnant. Rest assured I wasn't, but in a way writing the book has been a pregnancy of sorts. It was fun mostly, tiring sometimes, and exciting always. The result is my baby. I hope you love it as much as I do.

Favourite
Things in My Kitchen

Gas Stove

I converted to gas eight years ago when I renovated my kitchen. I would rather give up my car than give up my gas stove. If you are considering a kitchen renovation, write *gas stove* down at the top of your list. The instantaneous control of heat is the absolute best.

Heavy–Duty Pots and Pans

I'm not allowed to mention brand names, but my orange, cast-iron, enamel-coated cookware is amazing. I've had these pots for 25 years and they are still as good as new. Okay, they're slightly beat up, but still in excellent working order. They hold the heat well and I like the fact that they are so heavy. I think one of the reasons I have great biceps is that I haul those pots out a couple of times a day! Whatever cookware you decide on, buy top quality. It's worth it in the long run.

Food Processor

I don't use a food processor for soups, but I do use it a lot for grating and grinding, or puréeing my sorbets.

Mixmaster

My parents gave me a Mixmaster when I graduated with a degree in home economics from the University of British Columbia in 1976. I've dropped it at least 37 times, but it's still going strong. A must-have when you bake as much as I do.

Parchment Paper

Parchment paper has made scrubbing a cookie sheet unnecessary. I love parchment paper probably more than I love a couple of ex-boyfriends. Run out and buy a six-pack—it'll last a year. Warning: Don't substitute wax paper for parchment unless a recipe says you may.

Favourite Gadgets

Hand Blender

This is a dandy little gadget that purées soup right in the pot. You don't have to mess up your food processor or blender dumping hot soup into it (I always spill most of the soup, anyway). It's light, easy to use, and clean, and a must in my kitchen.

Zester

It's used to cut threadlike strips of zest from citrus fruits. The zester removes only the flavourful outer portion, leaving the bitter pith (white stuff) behind.

Juicer

I've got the old-fashioned kind your mom had. Cut citrus fruit in half. Press and twist on the juicer for instant fresh juice plus pulp. I bought mine at a garage sale for fifteen cents.

Paring Knife
Use this small, short-bladed knife to cut smaller things like carrots and fruit, and to core apples.

Measuring Spoons
I have eight sets, some metal and some plastic. I believe you can never have enough.

Chocolate Grater
I use this for grating chocolate right onto a cake, a cookie, or in my coffee. Handy and small and very convenient.

Garlic Press
Julia Child always mashes and minces her garlic with a knife. My apologies to the Great Dame of Cooking—I love my garlic press. There's less mess and this baby really does the trick.

Left–Handed Potato Peeler
What can I say? I'm left handed and I can't use the right-handed kind.

Cocoa Whisk
This mini-sized wire whisk whips up the cocoa powder and liquid without lumps. I couldn't live without it.

Honing Stone
A good cook has good knives. A great cook has sharp ones. I sharpen my knives all the time.

Nutmeg Grater
I bought my nutmeg grater at the Tin Shop at Ontario's Black Creek Pioneer Village. It grates whole nutmeg to give you the freshest flavour possible.

The Well-Stocked Kitchen

I have a well-stocked kitchen. I like knowing that on any given night six people could show up unexpectly for dinner and I could wow them in an hour. Here's my list. It may seem long, but even in my small kitchen, everything fits.

Baking Ingredients
All-purpose flour
Almond extract
Baking powder
Baking soda
Bitter-sweet chocolate
Bran (store in fridge)
Brown sugar
Cake and pastry flour
Chocolate cookie crumbs
Cocoa powder
Coconut
Corn syrup
Cornstarch
Currants
Gelatin
Icing sugar
Lard
Molasses

Pure vanilla extract

Raisins

Rolled oats—old fashioned and
  quick-cooking

Semi-sweet chocolate

Semi-sweet chocolate chips

Shortening

Unsweetened chocolate

Wheat germ (store in fridge)

White sugar

Whole wheat flour

Other Ingredients

Apple cider vinegar

Balsamic vinegar

Basmati rice

Bulgur

Canned black beans

Canned chicken stock

Canned kidney beans

Canned plum tomatoes

Canned tomato paste

Canned water-packed tuna

Canola oil

Converted rice

Couscous

Crackers

Dried beans

Hot chili oil

Jam

Liquid honey

Long-grain brown rice

Maple syrup

Marinated artichoke hearts

Marmalade

Olive oil

Pasta—all shapes

Peanut butter

Plain cookies

Red wine vinegar

Rice vinegar

Sesame oil

Short-grain brown rice

Split peas

White vinegar

Wild rice

Refrigerated Ingredients

Butter (If a recipe calls for unsalted butter,
  use unsalted butter. It contains less
  water than salted butter and really
  makes a difference in the outcome of a
  recipe.)

Chili sauce

Cream cheese

Dijon mustard

Eggs

Fish sauce

Fruits

Hazelnuts

Hot peppers

Ketchup

Low-fat mayonnaise

Mayonnaise

Milk (soy or cow's)

Olives

Oyster sauce

Pecans

Salsa
Soy sauce
Sun-dried tomatoes
Vegetables
Walnuts
Worcestershire sauce

Herbs and Spices

They don't stay fresh forever. If you can't remember the last time you used an herb or a spice, throw it out. Save the bottle, go to the bulk store, and buy a little more.

Allspice
Basil (I prefer fresh, but I dry mine and use it crumbled until my summer crop comes up.)
Black pepper
Cayenne
Chives (I grow four different kinds so I am partial to them.)
Cinnamon sticks
Curry powder

Dill
Dried oregano
Dried rosemary
Dried thyme
Garlic (I use fresh and powdered.)
Ginger (I use fresh and dried.)
Ground cinnamon
Ground cloves
Ground coriander
Ground cumin
Mint (I grow my own.)
Nutmeg (I use only the whole ones. I use a nutmeg grater.)
Paprika
Sage
Salt
Tarragon (I grow my own and dry it as well.)
Turmeric
White pepper

Methods and Techniques

I use the following methods and techniques in this book:

Beating Egg Whites

If you have a copper bowl, I'm very jealous. Copper really does make beating egg whites faster and better. If you don't have a copper bowl, use a glass or a metal bowl but *never use a plastic one*. When a recipe calls for *foamy*, think sea foam or soap bubbles. *Soft peak* means the egg whites should make a peak when you pull the beater out, and then the peak should flop over. Think of a melting soft ice cream cone. *Stiff peak* means the egg whites should make a peak and the peak should look like a tiny Mount Everest. When I taught high school home economics, I'd hold the bowl upside down over my head. Stiff peaks never fell on my head!

Blanching

To blanch, plunge fruits or vegetables into boiling water for a few minutes; once parboiled, remove fruits or vegetables and rinse with cold water to stop the cooking process.

Boiling

Boil liquid when food has to be cooked quickly. The surface will be full of bubbles breaking. You need to recognize boiling so that you'll know when you are simmering or poaching.

Creaming

When I say to cream the fat and sugar together, you need to beat the ingredients together until the mixture is smooth, soft, and creamy.

Segmenting

I use a lot of citrus segments. Here is my handy dandy method: Slice the top and bottom off the orange (so it won't roll around on the board). Use a sharp paring knife to cut off all the peel and pith. Now, hold the orange in one hand over a bowl. Use the same paring knife to cut down along the membrane on each side to remove the segment. The idea is to cut all the segments away from the membrane, so keep cutting down the sides of the membranes to remove all the segments. After all the fruit has been cut away, you'll be left with only the membrane.

Poaching

Poaching is the slow, gentle cooking of food in a liquid. The liquid at poaching temperature is barely bubbling.

Puréeing

Puréeing is the same as pulverizing: it means to grind or mash until you have a thick, smooth consistency. I purée soups and sorbets in the book, using a hand blender or food processor.

Reducing

Reducing means literally "to lose weight." In culinary terms it means to boil a liquid so that evaporation occurs. You are left with less liquid and a thicker, more flavourful mixture. Too bad it doesn't work on thighs!

Sautéing

Sautéing is cooking in a pan or pot with little fat at a high temperature. *Sauté* is the French word for "toss or jump." When you sauté, you need to stir occasionally so the food won't burn.

Simmering

Simmering is cooking food in a liquid so gently that tiny bubbles are just breaking the surface.

Tasting

Sneak a little taste before serving so you can adjust seasonings. This is also a great way to gain weight. I must have had a billion tastes while writing this book!

Whipping Cream

Make sure the beaters and bowl are freezing cold—put them in the freezer for 20 minutes—before whipping the cream. Cream just whips better when it's really cold. Never ever put the whipping cream in the freezer because you'll ruin it.

Zesting

Buy a zester. (See "Favourite Gadgets," page 3.) To zest means to remove the thin flavourful outer peel from citrus fruit. By doing this you get all the great taste with none of the bitter pith.

Glossary of Ingredients

Apple Cider Vinegar is made from fermented apple cider; it's fruity and has a clearer, lighter taste than other vinegars.

Balsamic Vinegar, which is available in most grocery shops, is a fabulous Italian vinegar that is aged in barrels for several years. A true balsamic should be aged for at least 3 to 5 years and have the word "Modena" on the label. (I once tasted a balsamic vinegar that was 50 years old—it was amazing! In Modena, some vintages are as old as 150 years.)

Butter—I almost exclusively use unsalted butter. I like the flavour and the freedom to add salt if I wish. As a general rule, you can substitute salted butter for unsalted in a savoury dish. But when it comes to baking, if a recipe specfies unsalted, please use it.

Chèvre or Goat Cheese, a tart cheese made from goat's milk, ranges from fresh and soft to dry and crumbly. I love its sharp, tangy flavour and usually buy it in tubes; at room temperature, it's creamy, soft and lovely.

Chicken Stock? Okay, I admit it: I use canned chicken stock. When I do have the time, I'll make a strong chicken stock, but for convenience *and* flavour, I buy Campbell's!

Coconut Milk is made made from shredded cocount and water. The canned variety is available in the Asian food section of most grocery stores, or in any Asian store. It comes in a light or low-fat version.

Feta Cheese is a classic Greek cheese traditionally made from goat's or sheep's milk. Today it is mostly made from cow's milk. It is cured and stored in a salty whey and has a rich, salty, tangy flavour.

Fish Sauce or Nam Pla is a salty fermented fish sauce used as a seasoning ingredient in Thai cooking. It is available in most grocery stores in the Asian food section.

Garam Masala is a hot, spicy mixture of ground spices that is used in Indian cooking. It is available in most grocery stores in the International food section or in any Indian store.

Ground Turkey or Chicken—I like the lighter flavours of these two ground meats. Look for the lean or extra lean varieties.

Kalamata Olives are dark, almost purple Greek olives. They are rich and fruity tasting and are usually sold in bulk in vats of olive oil. I live close to a "Greek village" in Toronto so I can always get fresh kalamata olives. Most grocery stores now carry them in their deli section.

Mango Chutney, available in the International food section of most groceries, is a sweet and spicy condiment that is as thick as jam. It is often used in Indian cooking, as an accompaniment to curried dishes.

Marinated Artichoke Hearts, in jars or canned, are found in the pickle section of most grocery stores.

Phyllo Pastry is very thin layers of pastry which, when baked, are transformed into delicate, flaky leaves. Used often in Greek cuisine, phyllo is available in the freezer section in most grocery stores.

Pickled Hot Pepper Rings, made from red or yellow peppers, are available in jars, in the pickle section of most grocery stores.

Roasted Red Peppers can be found in jars, in the pickle section of most grocery stores. During red pepper season, from late August to September, I usually buy a bushel basket, roast the peppers, then freeze them in small batches.

Sun-dried Tomatoes can be bought dried or reconstituted and preserved in seasoned oil. The dried version makes a great, healthy snack; the oily version doesn't! However, the sun-dried tomatoes in oil usually have a better flavour. Experiment and see which you prefer.

Appetizers

Appetizers such as my Peppercorn Pâté are supposed to excite your palate, tease your taste buds, and make you want more. Wow! (Too bad this appetizer wasn't a guy.)

Appetizers are an integral part of the meal but shouldn't be the entire meal. I think most people's biggest dinner-party mistake is to serve too many appetizers. When this happens, hungry guests overdo it before the meal, and that $48 salmon fillet just sits on stuffed people's plates.

So think small and intriguing, and whet—don't kill—your guests' appetites.

Appetizers

eppercorn Pâté

Serves 8–10

A couple of years ago I discovered a pure chicken-liver pâté at my favourite cheese shop on the Danforth in Toronto. Once I tasted the peppery richness, I was hooked. I could feel my arteries clogging with cholesterol, but I didn't care. One day, in a pâté daze, I realized that I could probably duplicate the recipe. I tried and tried and tried, and finally I did it.

Now I can make peppercorn pâté for half the price. Hey, does that make me a pâté dealer?

But eater beware: although this pâté is loaded in nutrients, it also contains a lot of bad cholesterol. So treat pâté like a special-occasion food: eat it only once in awhile.

¼ cup	unsalted butter	50 mL
1	large Spanish onion, finely chopped	1
3	cloves garlic, coarsely chopped	3
1 lb	organic chicken livers,* chopped	500 g
1 tbsp	chopped fresh tarragon OR 1 tsp/5 mL dried	15 mL
2 tbsp	crushed black peppercorns	25 mL
1 tsp	salt	5 mL
¼ tsp	white pepper	1 mL
¼ tsp	cayenne	1 mL
¼ cup	port	50 mL

1. In a large frying pan, melt the butter and sauté onion until translucent.

2. Add the garlic and chicken livers to the pan. Gently sauté until liver is no longer pink.

3. Add the tarragon, 1 tablespoon (15 mL) of the crushed peppercorns, salt, white pepper, and cayenne. Sauté 1 more minute.

4. Spoon into a food processor or blender. Pulse until smooth. Add the port and pulse again for 2 to 3 minutes.

5. Spoon into a crock or medium-sized bowl. Sprinkle remaining crushed peppercorns on top and refrigerate, covered, overnight. (This pâté really tastes better the next day, so curb the desire to sneak a taste until tomorrow.)

6. Serve with crusty bread, cream crackers, or melba toast.

> ✳ *The liver is the body's cleaning system. Antibiotics, chemicals, and so on are stored in the liver. I like to cook with chicken livers because the livers are so young they don't have time to absorb many antibiotics or chemicals that may be in their feed. Organic chicken livers are even better because they are from chickens that aren't fed anything containing antibiotics or chemicals.*

arinated Mushrooms

Serves 6–8

These babies cost a fortune to buy but only pennies to make. Okay, more like a couple of bucks, but the point is they are cheaper and taste a lot better than any store-bought kind I've ever had.

¼ cup	apple cider vinegar	50 mL
½ cup	balsamic vinegar	125 mL
½ cup	olive oil	125 mL
2 tbsp	water	25 mL
1 tbsp	dried basil	15 mL
1 tsp	dried thyme	5 mL
2	cloves garlic, mashed	2
1 tbsp	maple syrup	15 mL
40	small button mushrooms	40

1. In a 4-cup (1 L) jar with a tight-fitting lid, combine the apple cider vinegar, balsamic vinegar, olive oil, water, basil, thyme, garlic, and maple syrup.

2. Add the mushrooms. Screw on the lid and give it a shake.

3. Marinate in the fridge for 3 to 10 days. Give it a little shake every day. Walk the dog; shake the mushrooms.

4. Serve, drained, on a bed of lettuce. Have toothpicks on hand.

Salsa

Serves 6–8

"Home-made salsa? Has she lost her mind? It's easier to buy!" Well, try my home-made version during peak tomato season (July to September), and kiss off the commercial kind of salsa until October.

8	really ripe tomatoes, seeded and coarsely chopped	8
8	green onions, coarsely chopped	8
5	cloves garlic, minced (WOW!)	5
¼ cup	olive oil	50 mL
2 tsp	red wine vinegar	10 mL
¼ cup	pickled hot pepper rings,* chopped	50 mL
½ cup	chopped fresh cilantro	125 mL
1	fresh jalapeño pepper, seeded and chopped** (optional)	1
	Couple of dashes of Tabasco (optional)	

1. In a medium-sized, non-metallic bowl, mix together the tomatoes, green onions, garlic, olive oil, red wine vinegar, hot pepper rings, and cilantro. Add the jalapeño and Tabasco, if you are using, and mix well.

2. Let sit at room temperature for 30 minutes.

3. Drain off liquid. (I like to get rid of the extra liquid so the salsa is not watery and it's easier to eat on corn chips.)

4. Speaking of which, serve with corn chips.

> ❋ Pickled hot pepper rings can be purchased in most grocery stores, in the pickle section. I buy Unico's Pickled Hot Pepper Rings.
>
> ❋❋ Wear rubber gloves when handling hot chili peppers such as jalapeños, and don't forget to wash your hands thoroughly with soap and water before touching your eyes or mouth.

uickies

Serves 6–10

Oh, well—the title says it all. This snack's quick to make and extremely fun to eat.

1	jar (6 oz/170 mL) marinated artichoke hearts, drained	1
10	sun-dried tomatoes in oil, drained	10
2	cloves garlic, peeled	2
8 oz	soft, plain goat cheese (chèvre), at room temperature, cut in ¼-inch slices	220 g

Substitution No goat cheese kicking around the house? Okay, you can substitute cream cheese.

1. In a food processor, pulse together the artichoke hearts, sun-dried tomatoes, and garlic until the garlic is well incorporated.

2. Arrange the sliced goat cheese on a small platter. Spoon the artichoke mixture over top. Serve with crackers.

heese Pâté

Here are two cheese pâté recipes: one for lovers of mould—I mean, Gorgonzola cheese—and one for everyone else.

Cheese Pâté with Gorgonzola

4 oz	cream cheese, at room temperature	125 g
1 oz	strong white Cheddar, grated	30 g
4 oz	Gorgonzola, crumbled	125 g
Pinch	red pepper flakes	Pinch
½ cup	chopped walnuts	125 mL

1. In a food processor or blender, pulse together the cream cheese, white Cheddar, Gorgonzola, and red pepper flakes until smooth.

2. Now the messy part: on a piece of parchment or wax paper, sprinkle the walnuts. Use a rubber spatula to scoop out the cheese mixture. Shape it into a log using your hands—yuck!—and roll on the walnut-sprinkled parchment paper until it is completely covered with nuts.

3. Wrap in parchment paper or plastic wrap and refrigerate until one hour before serving. (The cheese tastes best at room temperature.) Serve with crackers.

Cheese Pâté without Gorgonzola

4 oz	cream cheese, at room temperature	125 g
2 oz	strong white Cheddar, grated	50 g
¼ tsp	red pepper flakes	1 mL
½ cup	chopped fresh cilantro or parsley	125 mL

1. In a food processor or blender, pulse together the cream cheese, Cheddar, and red pepper flakes until smooth.

2. Sprinkle the chopped cilantro or parsley on a piece of parchment or wax paper. Scoop out the cheese mixture with a rubber spatula and shape it into a log with your hands. (Food therapy!) Roll until the cheese log is completely covered with herbs.

3. Wrap in parchment paper or plastic wrap and refrigerate until one hour before serving. (The cheese tastes best at room temperature.) Serve with crackers.

Asparagus with Lime Mayonnaise

Serves 4–8

I don't have an asparagus pot. I don't know anyone who does. The only person I've seen with one is that blonde woman who has her own show—her name escapes me.

Anyway, the rest of us can use my kind of asparagus pot: a frying pan with a lid.

2 lb	asparagus	1 kg
½ cup	mayonnaise	125 mL
	(regular or low-fat)	
	Zest of 1 lime	
	Juice of 1 lime	

1. Break off the ends of the asparagus. Do this by holding an asparagus stalk with two hands and snapping off the woody part just where it meets the green part. It's a feel—you'll get the hang of it. Think snappy sound.

2. Cover the asparagus with water. Bring to a boil, cover, and *gently* boil for 4 to 5 minutes.

3. Drain the asparagus and plunge it into ice-cold water. (This will stop the asparagus from cooking.)

4. Remove to strainer once it is cool. Store, covered, in the fridge.

5. Meanwhile, mix together the mayonnaise, zest, and 2 tablespoons (25 mL) of the lime juice. Beat in 1 more tablespoon (15 mL) of lime juice, if desired. Chill.

6. To serve, arrange the asparagus on a platter and drizzle the lime mayonnaise over the tips.

Salads

When I was growing up, a salad was head lettuce, cucumber, and, if you were really lucky, a sorry-looking tomato. All of this was smothered in some kind of mayonnaise dressing. Well, that was then.

Today, my salads are combinations of radicchio, Oak leaf, spinach, Bibb, romaine, watercress, lamb's lettuce, and endive. Yes, I've come a long way in the greens department. Now, if I could just get this relationship issue worked out.

My dressings, too, are exciting and different. They range from garlicky vinaigrettes to exotic mango chutneys.

Salads should be an introduction to the much anticipated main course. Like the opening act at a rock concert, salad is great alone, but its main function is to warm up the audience for the entrée.

Salad Rules

1. Never buy greens that look brown or rusty. They'll turn into slime in a matter of days. Trust me—I am the slime police.

2. Wash and spin the greens dry. Wrap them in paper towels, put them into a plastic bag, and store in the fridge. They should stay perfect for at least two days.

(No salad spinner? Place greens in a clean tea towel. Hold ends together tightly. Go outside and whip it around your head, yelling "Yee ha" like a ranch hand in a rodeo. Centrifugal force is an amazing thing. Caution: do not let go of the tea towel until it has come to a complete stop!)

3. Don't chop up lettuce. Gently tear it into bite-sized pieces. Remember an age-old culinary rule: no one likes to eat anything bigger than his or her head.

4. Put the dressing on just before serving unless the recipe tells you differently. This will prevent limp salads.

Salads

ew Wave Spinach Salad

Serves 4

Where's the bacon, the croutons, the thick and fat gunked-up dressing? Gone, gone, gone. Say goodbye to the old version and try my new wave.

Greens

1	bunch baby spinach (or enough to serve 4)	1
1	large sweet red pepper, julienned	1
1	Anjou or Bartlett pear, peeled, cored, and cut into 8 slices	1
¼ cup	walnut pieces	50 mL
4	thin slices red onion	4

Dressing

¼ cup	low-fat mayonnaise	50 mL
2 tbsp	apple cider vinegar	25 mL
1 tbsp	maple syrup	15 mL

1. Wash and dry the spinach. Refrigerate in a plastic bag.

2. In a small bowl, whisk together the low-fat mayonnaise, apple cider vinegar, and maple syrup.

3. When ready to serve, toss the spinach and red pepper with the dressing.

4. Divide the salad equally among four plates.

5. Arrange the slices of pear on top.

6. Sprinkle the walnuts on top of each salad and garnish with the red onion.

7. Serve immediately and get ready to give away the recipe.

> **Note** You can double or even triple this recipe—lightly toss instead of serving on individual plates.

Lick the Spoon!

Romaine with Avocado Dressing

Serves 4–8

I love "trying out" new recipes. I think it's the non-committal aspect of "trying out" I like the best. If I don't like the recipe, no big deal—I haven't lost a lot, nobody got hurt, and it didn't take up much of my time. Hey, if I really wanted to, I'd fix it.

Wouldn't it be nice to be able to apply this "trying out" thing to . . . say . . . someone you'd like to date?

Try this one out—it's a keeper.

Greens

1	large head romaine lettuce	1

Dressing

2 tbsp	olive oil	25 mL
2 tbsp	lime juice	25 mL
1 tbsp	plain yogurt	15 mL
1 tbsp	mayonnaise	15 mL
¼	ripe avocado	¼
1	clove garlic, mashed	1
1 tsp	Worcestershire sauce	5 mL
½ tsp	chili powder	2 mL

1. Wash and dry the romaine. Place in a plastic bag and refrigerate.

2. Purée the olive oil, lime juice, yogurt, mayonnaise, avocado, garlic, Worcestershire, and chili powder.

3. When ready to serve, tear the romaine into bite-sized pieces and toss with dressing. (You don't have to use all the salad dressing—use only as much as you want.)

ixed Baby Greens with Mango Chutney Dressing

Serves 6–8

This is a very exotic salad dressing. It is not for everyone. My 70-year-old parents thought it was very weird, and my "foodie" friends loved it. So I feel that the best thing to do is to ask this exotic, revealing question (sort of a salad screening test): "If you were stranded on a desert island, who would you like to be stranded with?" If the answer is "Walter Cronkite," don't serve it.

Greens

If possible, use mesclun mix—a gourmet mixture of baby greens. You can buy it already washed in most supermarkets or specialty grocery stores. It's fairly pricey, so you might want to make your own. If you do, combine baby spinach, endive, lamb's lettuce, Oak leaf, Bibb, and beet greens. Use 1 cup per serving.

Dressing

½ cup	extra virgin olive oil	125 mL
¼ cup	lemon juice	50 mL
2 tbsp	apple cider vinegar	25 mL
¼ cup	mango chutney	50 mL
1 tsp	curry powder	5 mL
¼ tsp	turmeric	1 mL
Pinch	cayenne	Pinch
½ tsp	white sugar	2 mL

1. If you are using store-bought mesclun, store in fridge. If you are making your own, wash and thoroughly dry the greens. Refrigerate in a plastic bag.

2. Purée the olive oil, lemon juice, apple cider vinegar, mango chutney, curry powder, turmeric, cayenne, and sugar. Store in the fridge until show time.

3. When you're ready to serve, ask the exotic, revealing question. Based on the answer, either toss with dressing, and serve, or offer a sliced tomato.

# reens and Grapefruit

Serves 4–6

This salad is the perfect way to jog your taste buds. I usually serve this in February, when my entire body needs a wake-up call.

Greens

8	leaves romaine lettuce	8
½	bunch watercress	½
	(or roughly 6 stalks)	
2	celery stalks, thinly sliced	2

Dressing

1	large ruby red grapefruit	1
1 tbsp	olive oil	15 mL
1 tbsp	red wine vinegar	15 mL
1 tsp	Dijon mustard	5 mL
1 tsp	liquid honey	5 mL
1	shallot, minced	1

1. Wash and dry the romaine and watercress. Refrigerate in a plastic bag.

2. Cut off the peel, and section the grapefruit (see Methods and Techniques). Squeeze the juice from the remaining centre section (call it the core and membrane, if you want to be technical). Reserve juice.

3. Whisk together the olive oil, red wine vinegar, Dijon mustard, and honey.

4. Add the shallot and the grapefruit juice you "reserved." (What an interesting culinary term for saved.)

5. Tear the romaine into bite-sized pieces.

6. Toss together the romaine, watercress, and celery with the dressing. Place the grapefruit sections on top and serve immediately.

Caesar Salad

**Serves 2 as a main course,
4–6 as an appetizer**

Here's a bit of trivia: Julius Caesar hated anchovies. He felt they inhibited his sexual performance during the famous Roman orgies. The original Caesar salad didn't have any anchovies. Unfortunately, these bits of scintillating trivia are absolutely irrelevant because it was restaurateur Caesar Cardini who invented this famous salad, in 1924—not amorous Julius, in 40 B.C.

Caesar salad should be garlicky and crisp, with just a hint of dressing. I'm sure Signor Cardini would approve of my low-fat version.

Greens

1	large head romaine lettuce	1

Dressing

1	very fresh large egg	1
3	cloves garlic	3
2 tbsp	olive oil	25 mL
Pinch	salt	Pinch
¼ tsp	dry mustard	1 mL
1 tsp	Worcestershire sauce	5 mL
	Juice of one lemon	
	(2–3 tbsp/ 25–45 mL)	
½ cup	freshly grated	125 mL
	Romana cheese	

1. Wash and dry the romaine. Refrigerate in a plastic bag.

2. Coddle the egg: boil it in the shell for 1 minute or microwave a shelled egg for 30 seconds on Medium. Either way, you want the white slightly cooked.

3. In a large salad bowl, mash together the garlic and oil until the mixture is thick and pasty looking.

4. Beat the coddled egg into the garlic mixture.

5. Stir in the salt, dry mustard, and Worcestershire.

6. *Slowly*, beat in the lemon juice.

7. Gently tear your crunchy romaine into bite-sized pieces.

8. Toss the romaine with the dressing.

9. Sprinkle on the Romana cheese. Toss again and serve immediately.

> **Pitfall** *The dressing is thin and liquidy. You didn't* **slowly** *beat in the lemon juice. If you just dump it in, the oil will separate and leave you a less-than-perfect dressing. The plus—it'll still taste great. Do it right the next time.*

M air's House Salad

Serves 4–6

What can I say? I really like naming things after myself. I would have been a great dictator.

Greens

1	head Bibb lettuce	1
4	radicchio leaves	4
4	arugula leaves	4

Dressing

¼ cup	balsamic vinegar	50 mL
¼ cup	olive oil	50 mL
2 tbsp	Dijon mustard	25 mL
2	cloves garlic, minced	2

1. Wash and dry the greens. Refrigerate in a plastic bag.

2. Whisk together the balsamic vinegar, olive oil, Dijon mustard, and garlic. Store in a glass jar with a tight-fitting lid in the refrigerator.

3. When ready to serve, tear the greens into bite-sized pieces.

4. Shake the dressing and pour over the greens. Toss and serve immediately.

Pea Salad

Serves 4–6

How many times have you opened up the vegetable drawer of the fridge to discover a barely recognizable head of smelly, slimy lettuce? Didn't read note 1 in the "Salad Rules" (page 21), right? Hey, who knew lettuce didn't last six weeks?

Well, I've come up with a solution to slime. Make a salad without lettuce! Yes—use frozen peas and sweet red peppers.

2½ cups	frozen peas	625 mL
1	large sweet red pepper, julienned	1
¼ cup	olive oil	50 mL
1 tbsp	white wine vinegar	15 mL
2 tbsp	apple cider vinegar	25 mL
1 tbsp	Russian-style mustard*	15 mL
¼ cup	finely chopped parsley	50 mL
1	shallot, minced	1

1. Rinse the peas in a colander under cold water until they feel less like frozen peas and more like fresh ones!

2. Whisk together the olive oil, white wine vinegar, apple cider vinegar, and Russian-style mustard.

3. Stir in the parsley and shallots.

4. Toss the thawed peas and red peppers with dressing. Serve immediately.

***** *Russian-style mustard is like a sweet Dijon mustard. Try the President's Choice version.*

Lick the Spoon!

Baby Spinach with Spicy Vinaigrette

Serves 4

This salad—meant for garlic lovers or vampire fighters—has a definite kick to it.

Enjoy it with friends but never eat it on Valentine's Day or before an important rendezvous or a job interview. You'll find yourself all alone and/or without a career!

Greens

1	bunch baby spinach (or enough to serve 4)	1

Dressing

⅓ cup	olive oil	75 mL
⅓ cup	apple cider vinegar	75 mL
2	cloves garlic, crushed	2
⅓ cup	coarsely chopped pickled hot pepper rings*	75 mL

1. Wash and dry the spinach. Place in plastic bag and refrigerate.

2. Whisk together the olive oil, apple cider vinegar, and garlic.

3. Stir in the hot pepper rings.

4. Toss the spinach with the dressing. Serve immediately. Wow! Garlicky!

❋ Wear rubber gloves when handling hot chili peppers such as jalapeños, and don't forget to wash your hands thoroughly with soap and water before touching your eyes or mouth.

ucumber Salad

This is a two-way salad. You serve it either on a bed of crispy romaine lettuce or as a side dish for a fish entrée.

Make this salad one day ahead, or at least one hour before serving.

¼ cup	rice vinegar	50 mL
3 tbsp	warm water	45 mL
2 tbsp	white sugar	25 mL
½ tsp	red pepper flakes	2 mL
1	shallot, minced	1
1	English cucumber, thinly sliced	1

1. In a small bowl, whisk together the rice vinegar, warm water, sugar, and red pepper flakes.

2. Stir in the shallot.

3. Pour over the cucumber. Cover and refrigerate until ready to serve.

Pitfall *The salad tastes like metal. You used a metal bowl to store the salad in. Whenever the dressing contains vinegar, use a glass, Corning Ware, or plastic container. Throw the metallic-tasting salad out and start over.*

Potato Salad

Serves 4-8

Okay, so there isn't any lettuce in this recipe. I was really torn, no pun intended, as to where potato salad should be. Is it a vegetable? or a salad? I asked my friends, but they were no help at all. So I made an executive decision: it's a greenless salad.

20	new red potatoes	20
6 tbsp	balsamic vinegar	90 mL
1 tbsp	grainy Dijon mustard	15 mL
1	shallot, minced	1
6	radishes, thinly sliced	6
2	celery stalks, thinly sliced	2
½ cup	chopped fresh chives	125 mL

1. Boil whole potatoes until tender, about 20 minutes. Drain and set aside.

2. In a large bowl, whisk together the vinegar and mustard.

3. Mix in the shallot, radishes, and celery.

4. Cut the potatoes in half and add to the dressing and other vegetables.

5. Sprinkle the chives on top and stir once more until combined.

6. Here's your big choice: serve immediately, while slightly hot, or refrigerate until serving time and eat it cold. Either way it's great and it's fat free. So indulge.

Soups

Soups should warm the stomach as well as the soul. I remember watching an episode of the seventies TV sitcom "All in the Family" in which Archie Bunker sat down to what he thought was a nice bowl of hot potato soup. He gave it a couple of cooling blows, took a taste, and exclaimed, "Ah, what kind of soup is this? Three blows and it's cold?" Well, so much for vichyssoise. I'm with Archie—soup should be hot.

Soup Rules

1. Purée—I have a hand blender that I just stick into the pot. It's an amazing gadget. If you don't have one, rush out and purchase one or put it on your wish list.

2. All soups taste better the next day. Make the day before you serve it or double the recipe and serve it again a couple of days later.

3. I don't use a lot of salt or pepper. So, if you find these recipes not tuned up to your palate, you can always add some. I just don't like salt much—except on potatoes! Love it on spuds.

4. I usually use unsalted butter. If the recipe calls for *butter*, use salted or regular butter. If it says *unsalted butter*, use unsalted.

5. If you are watching your cholesterol levels, substitute olive oil (contains monosaturated fats that can help reduce bad cholesterol, or LDL, leaving the good cholesterol, HDL, intact) for butter, and evaporated skim milk for cream.

ucchini Soup

Serves 4

My parents grew tomatoes, corn, carrots, beets, green beans, cucumbers, and raspberries in our Vancouver backyard. They worked the soil, adding the two C's and the one M—chicken and cow manure with just enough mushroom manure—to really stink up the yard. Then there was the pièce de résistance—their precious compost. (My parents were organic farmers and they didn't even know it.) We had a compost bin the size of an Austin Mini. And it was pretty soft to land on, as I discovered the time I jumped off the garage roof on a dare.

The first thing I did when I got my own backyard was plant a vegetable garden. But I decided to break from family tradition and plant different stuff. I carefully seeded for broccoli, cauliflower, lettuce, kale, and zucchini.

That fateful summer, the zucchini choked the living daylights out of everything. I swear the stuff grew three feet a night, sneaking up on the unassuming broccoli and strangling it at dawn. Who knew 20 seeds would yield 47,003 zucchini? They ought to put a warning on the package.

Well, being resourceful and the child of parents brought up during the Depression, I became a culinary zucchini expert. As a living testament, here is one of my favourite zucchini recipes.

1 tbsp	butter	15 mL
1	medium onion, chopped	1
2	cloves garlic, minced	2
3 cups	chicken stock	750 mL
4	medium zucchini, chopped (approx. 1¼ lb/625 g)	4
½ cup	35% whipping cream	125 mL
½ tsp	salt	2 mL
¼ tsp	white pepper	1 mL

1. In a medium-sized pot, sauté the onion and garlic in the butter until tender, 3 to 4 minutes.

2. Add the stock and zucchini. Bring to a boil, reduce to simmer, and cover. Simmer until the zucchini is soft, 30 to 40 minutes. Purée. You can prepare the soup to this step ahead of time and either refrigerate or freeze. Then proceed to step 3.

3. Either bring the soup back to simmer or continue from step 2. Add the cream, salt, and pepper. Heat through and serve immediately.

> **Note** *Don't substitute black pepper for white. Your guests will think you burnt the soup.*

uick Black Bean Soup

Serves 2–4

Cooking with beans doesn't have to be a precision-timing affair. So many of my friends use the old line "I haven't got the time to cook them." Hey, you don't have to soak them overnight! Who knew? Yes . . . you can buy beans that are canned. Even black beans.

This recipe calls for, you guessed it, canned black beans. This soup takes all of 25 minutes to cook. Hey, by the time you've read the mail, looked at your kids' homework, and yelled at the dog, supper's ready.

1 cup	chicken stock	250 mL
1	medium onion, diced	1
1	can (19 oz / 540 mL) black beans (don't drain)	1
1½ tsp	ground cumin	7 mL
1½ tsp	ground coriander	7 mL
½ cup	low-fat yogurt (optional)	125 mL
¼ cup	chopped fresh cilantro (optional)	50 mL

1. In a medium-sized pot, heat the chicken stock, onion, and black beans. Bring to a boil, cover and simmer for 20 minutes or until the onions are soft and the beans are heated through.

2. Purée.

3. Stir in the cumin and coriander. Purée once more.

4. Ladle into bowls. If desired, add 2 tablespoons (25 mL) of the yogurt to each bowl—watch it sink—and sprinkle 1 tablespoon (15 mL) of the cilantro. Serve with a green salad and wholegrain bread.

ild Mushroom Soup

Serves 4

I was first introduced to foraging for wild mushrooms on an episode of "Harrowsmith Country Life." I went into the forests of New Brunswick and found chanterelle, oyster, and blue trumpet mushrooms. It was fun and easy, and a great day in the forest.

Well, back in Toronto, and with my hectic schedule, I occasionally stumble upon toadstools in my garden.

Lucky for me, my local grocer now regularly stocks wild mushrooms. Any time I want to forage city-style, I pack up and head to Loblaws.

2 tbsp	unsalted butter	25 mL
½ cup	minced shallots	125 mL
8 oz	wild mushrooms, chopped	250 g
2½ tbsp	all-purpose flour	37 mL
3½ cups	chicken stock	875 mL
¼ tsp	dried thyme	1 mL
¼ cup	dry sherry	50 mL
½ cup	35% whipping cream	125 mL

1. In a large pot, melt the butter and sauté the shallots and mushrooms about 5 minutes or until the shallots are translucent. Don't stir too often but watch that they don't burn.

2. Stir in the flour until it is well combined.

3. Pour in the stock and add the thyme. Bring to a boil. Reduce to simmer; cover and continue cooking for 1 hour.

4. You are only going to purée part of the soup so you'll have chunks of wild mushrooms and puréed bits. Remove ⅔ cup (150 mL) of the cooked mushrooms and stock. Purée.

5. Pour the purée back into the pot. Add the sherry; stir.

6. When the soup is simmering, add the cream, and stir. Serve immediately.

Note *Use any combination of wild mushrooms you have available.*

Broccoli Soup

Serves 4

How do you get kids to eat broccoli? Make it into a puréed soup. Then tell them this is the soup that Batman, Sailor Moon, or Polkaroo eats, and the next thing you know, they're eating it.

Unfortunately, this approach doesn't work on adults. My tack is to tell them to grow up and try something new for once in their lives. (Note: only works on close relatives. Not especially effective on bosses, neighbours, or anyone in uniform.)

4 cups	chicken stock	1 L
1	leek, white part only, chopped	1
2	cloves garlic, minced	2
1	bunch broccoli, chopped	1
¾ cup	evaporated skim milk	175 mL
¼ tsp	white pepper	1 mL

1. In a medium-sized pot, stir together the chicken stock, leek, garlic, and broccoli. Bring to a boil; reduce to simmer, cover, and continue simmering until the broccoli and leeks are soft, 30 to 40 minutes.

2. Purée the soup.

3. Increase heat and when the soup is simmering add the milk. Heat through. Season with the pepper. Serve immediately.

Note *Lactose intolerant? Substitute soy milk for skim milk.*

rench Onion Soup

Serves 4

Back in the seventies, French onion soup was on every bistro's menu. I always loved the bubbly bowls of soup that begged to be eaten slowly.

Believing I could make a soup that was better than those served up by my favourite bistros, into my kitchen I went. I substituted chicken stock for beef and quickly found that chicken stock gave the soup a more elegant flavour.

This great soup is only made greater if you are serving it by candlelight to a sexy Frenchman.

2 tbsp	olive oil	25 mL
1 tbsp	butter	15 mL
4	large onions, thinly sliced (use a food processor)	4
2 tbsp	all-purpose flour	25 mL
¼ tsp	salt	1 mL
Pinch	pepper	Pinch
1	clove garlic, minced	1
1 tbsp	chopped fresh parsley	15 mL
¼ tsp	dried thyme	1 mL
4 cups	chicken stock	1 L
1 cup	dry white wine	250 mL
8	slices baguette	8
2 tbsp	dry sherry	25 mL
¼ cup	freshly grated Parmesan cheese	50 mL
2 cups	grated Gruyère	500 mL

1. In a large pot, heat the oil and butter; toss in the onions and sauté until translucent, 5 to 7 minutes.

2. Add the flour and stir well to coat the onions.

3. Add the salt, pepper, garlic, fresh parsley, and thyme. Stir well.

4. Pour in the chicken stock and white wine. Cover and simmer for 45 minutes.

5. Meanwhile, in each of four onion-soup bowls, place one slice of bread in the bottom. That takes all of 1 minute. Go read a magazine.

6. Ding—45 minutes is over. Add the sherry to the soup. Stir. Ladle out the soup into the four bowls, making sure they all get about the same amount of onions. Turn on the broiler.

7. Sprinkle 1 tablespoon (15 mL) of the Parmesan cheese onto each bowl of soup. Drop on the second slice of bread and slightly submerge. Sprinkle ½ cup (125 mL) of the grated Gruyère on top of each bowl.

8. Broil until nice and bubbly brown. Serve.

9. Make sure you warn the guests: it's very hot!

10. Sit back and enjoy the raves.

inestrone

Serves 4–8

Minestrone is a very thick soup and I'm not kidding. This hearty, high-fibre version is thick enough to stand a spoon in.

1 tbsp	olive oil	15 mL
1	medium onion, chopped	1
2	cloves garlic, minced	2
⅓ cup	chopped celery	75 mL
1	large potato, peeled and chopped	1
1	large carrot, peeled and chopped	1
½	small head savoy cabbage, chopped	½
1 cup	chopped canned plum tomatoes OR 3 plum tomatoes, skinned and chopped*	250 mL
3 cups	home-made chicken stock OR 1 can (10 oz/284 mL) condensed, diluted	750 mL
2 cups	cooked red kidney beans OR 1 can (14 oz/398 mL), drained	500 mL
1 tbsp	chopped fresh basil	15 mL
½ cup	shell pasta	125 mL
	Salt and pepper	
	Freshly grated Parmesan cheese	

1. In a large pot, heat oil. Toss in onion and garlic and sauté for 3 minutes.

2. Add the celery, potato, carrot, and cabbage. Sauté for 3 more minutes.

3. Add the tomatoes, stock, beans, and basil. Simmer with the lid on for 30 minutes. Stir occasionally.

4. Add the pasta and simmer, covered, for 30 more minutes. Stir occasionally.

5. Season to taste with salt and pepper. If you want a stronger basil flavour, add more fresh basil.

6. When ready to serve, ladle into bowls and sprinkle with Parmesan cheese. I like about 2 tablespoons (25 mL) on mine. Serve with whole wheat bread, corn bread, or whole wheat scones.

> ***** *How to skin a tomato (or is it peel)? I call it **skinning** because I pour boiling water over top of them. The skins come off easily. **Peeling** to me means you use a peeler. So my book, my rules: it's called **skinning**.*

Butternut Squash Soup

Serves 4

In my West Coast opinion, squash is a very Ontarian vegetable. I've heard that this is because the pioneers lost all their squash seeds while crossing the treacherous Rockies. "Oh, darn, Elsie-May, there goes the wagon. Isn't that the one with all them squash seeds?"

Hence the reason most Vancouverites—at least the ones I know—have never eaten squash. (Okay, it may not be historically accurate, but it explains a lot.)

Well, I moved to Toronto and discovered that squash is a delicious, nutritious winter gourd. I serve this low-fat soup every autumn when the butternuts are at peak season.

1	large butternut squash	1
1 cup	finely chopped onion	250 mL
1 cup	chicken stock	250 mL
1 cup	unsweetened apple juice	250 mL
1 tbsp	curry powder	15 mL
1 cup	evaporated skim milk	250 mL

1. Microwave the squash on High for 10 to 20 minutes or until soft. Let cool for 20 minutes. (Cooling just makes it easier to handle. If you have non-heat-sensitive hands, forgo the cooling process.)

2. In a medium-sized pot, mix together the onion and chicken stock. Bring the liquid to a simmer and cook, covered, for 5 minutes.

3. Cut the squash in half; peel it, remove seeds, and coarsely chop the pulp.

4. Add the squash pulp to the onion and stock, along with the apple juice.

5. Continue to simmer, covered, until the squash is soft enough to purée.

6. Purée. Add the curry powder and simmer gently until ready to serve.

7. When all your guests are seated, add the evaporated skim milk. Stir until the soup is warmed through, about 2 minutes. Serve.

Note *If you are as skinny as a rail and have no concerns about fat, throw caution to the wind and substitute 1 cup (250 mL) of 35% whipping cream for the evaporated skim milk. And remember, deep down in my heart, I hate you!*

Pumpkin Soup with Fresh Ginger

Serves 4–6

A fall soup with a hint of ginger. Simple and low in fat.

1 tbsp	olive oil	15 mL
1 cup	diced onion	250 mL
2 cups	chicken stock	500 mL
1½ cups	canned pumpkin purée	375 mL
1½ tbsp	grated fresh ginger	22 mL
1 cup	evaporated skim milk	250 mL

1. In a medium-sized pot, heat the oil. Add onion and sauté until translucent, about 5 minutes.

2. Add the stock, pumpkin purée, and ginger. Bring to a boil. Reduce heat, cover, and simmer for 30 minutes.

3. Purée.

4. Add the evaporated skim milk. Do not boil; bring back to simmer. Serve immediately.

urried Chicken Soup

Serves 4–6

Chicken soup has been called the Jewish penicillin. My curried version is spicy nirvana. Just what the doctor ordered to unplug a stuffy nose.

1 tbsp	butter	15 mL
¾ cup	coarsely chopped onion	175 mL
1	large sweet red pepper, chopped	1
1	Granny Smith apple, peeled, cored, and chopped	1
1 tbsp	curry powder	15 mL
7 cups	chicken stock	1.75 L
⅓ cup	converted rice	75 mL
8 oz	boneless, skinless chicken breast, chopped into ½-inch (1cm) pieces	250 g
1 tsp	red pepper flakes	5 mL

1. In a medium-sized pot, heat butter. Add onion and sauté for 3 minutes or until translucent.

2. Add the red pepper and apple. Sauté for 3 more minutes or until the apple is soft.

3. Stir in the curry powder.

4. Add the chicken stock and rice. Bring to a boil, reduce heat, cover, and simmer for 20 minutes or until the rice is tender.

5. Add the chicken and continue to simmer, covered, until the chicken is cooked, 5 to 10 minutes.

6. Add the red pepper flakes, stir, and serve.

Vegetable Side Dishes

I was raised on five to six servings of vegetables per day. They were served pure and simple. It probably helped that my parents grew their own vegetables, making it an adventure to go out and pick which ones we were having for dinner.

Many a summer's supper was corn on the cob, new potatoes, carrots, beans, beet tops, sliced tomatoes, and cucumbers. Oh, and just for good measure, a small slice of chicken or beef.

I still believe in serving vegetables pure and simple. By and large I don't like dressing them up too much. I feel it's very important to be able to recognize the vegetable you are eating. You should say "the broccoli was great" instead of "I liked the green stuff with cheese sauce all over it." I'm not totally against camouflaging vegetables. It's just that I'm more for easy vegetable identification.

I think "Jeopardy" ought to have a category in which people taste a vegetable. "I'll take green cruciferous vegetables for $500, Alex." Munch, munch, munch. "What is celery?" Bad buzzer sound. "No, I'm sorry, Doris, celery isn't even close. It's kale." Now there's a fun vegetable show.

Vegetable Rules

1. Always buy what's in season. The chances of asparagus tasting great in September are pretty low. Buy your fill of asparagus when it is in season, anywhere from February to the end of June.

2. Buy what looks like it's still alive. A wilted head of Swiss chard just won't taste as good as a firm, brightly coloured one. Think of it in car terms: if money were no object, would you buy a shiny red one or a paint-rotting-off, awful-looking one? (Both have identical interiors.) You'd go with the shiny one, of course.

3. If there is any brown or yellow on broccoli, kale, Swiss chard, or any other green vegetable, don't buy it—it's old.

4. If possible, shop for vegetables two or three times a week. You'll have a better chance of buying fresh ones.

5. Store vegetables in the fridge, except potatoes, garlic, and onions. Tomatoes taste better at room temperature, but if they are getting too ripe, store them in the fridge.

6. Speaking of potatoes and onions, they taste great together, but they should never be stored together. The gas from the onions causes the potatoes to sprout eyes, which are a bad thing. (See note 7.)

7. Don't buy potatoes that have sprouting eyes or a green tinge. These potatoes contain toxic levels of solanine—they won't kill you, but I'd sure think twice about eating them. Okay, so you bought great-looking potatoes that turned green and sprouted eyes. Throw them out.

8. The general rule of thumb—bigger is better—is out, as far as vegetables go. Smaller means younger, which means sweeter and more tender. So don't go and buy a big honkin' turnip—the smaller ones will be better.

9. If possible, buy just-picked corn. From the moment corn is picked, it starts converting its sugar content to starch. So the longer it sits around, the starchier it gets.

10. Cook vegetables in the least amount of water possible and with the lid on. This will prevent leaching of vitamins C and B and dissipation of nutrients. In English, vegetables cooked in a lot of water won't be as good for you.

11. However (as soon as you write a rule, something comes along to break it), when boiling strong-flavoured vegetables such as cabbage or cauliflower, you will need more water.

12. Canada's Food Guide suggests five to ten servings of vegetables and fruit daily. So start eating. Get healthy. And think pure and simple.

russels Sprouts

Serves 4 Brussels sprout lovers, 20 abstainers

1 lb	small Brussels sprouts	500 g
1 tbsp	maple syrup	15 mL
1 tbsp	butter	15 mL

I always kid about my Grandma making her famous Sunday dinner—roast beef and Yorkshire pudding. We always ate at 6 p.m., so she would start the infamous "sprouts" at 3 p.m.! No wonder I never liked the grey, mushy blobs.

It wasn't until I was in university that I tasted a Brussels sprout that had been cooked the proper way. Who knew they were so good!

1. Wash the sprouts and cut off the woody stems.

2. Put in a large pot and barely cover with water.

3. Bring to a gentle boil, cover, and cook for 5 to 7 minutes or until tender. Take one out and taste it. Too hard? Cook a couple of minutes more.

4. Drain. Add the maple syrup and butter to the bright green Brussels sprouts.

5. Mix until coated and that's it! I'll say it again: some vegetables taste best when they haven't been done up too much.

**roccoli, Red Pepper, and Fresh Ginger**

Serves 4-6

Broccoli is one of the best all-round vegetables. It's rich in fibre so it may help prevent colon cancer. It contains many photochemicals, in particular indoles and isothiocyanates, which may help protect the body against other cancers.

All in all, it tastes great and it's good for you. So "eat your broccoli!"

1 tbsp	hot chili oil*	15 mL
1 lb	broccoli, cut into florets	500 g
1 tsp	grated fresh ginger	5 mL
¼ cup	water	50 mL
1	large sweet red pepper, sliced into strips	1

1. Heat a large frying pan or wok. Add the chili oil.

2. Add the broccoli. Stir-fry for 1 to 2 minutes.

3. Add the ginger and water. Put on the lid and cook for 2 to 3 minutes.

4. Add the red pepper, toss. Cover and cook for 1 to 2 more minutes. Serve immediately.

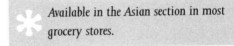 *Available in the Asian section in most grocery stores.*

Kale

Serves 4-6

How many times have you walked right past the kale in the produce department? Ever bought it? Know what it is? Well, it's a lowly member of the cabbage family that is full of vitamins A and C, folic acid, calcium, and iron.

The price is very reasonable, so live life on the razor's edge—shell out $1.79 and try kale. Choose one that has dark green leaves (it may have tinges of dark blue or purple), and store it in the coldest part of your fridge for up to three days. When you finally decide to cook it, cut off the stalks—these are too tough to eat. Try the recipe below for a slightly Asian flavour, or, if you prefer, cook as in the Swiss Chard recipe, on page 54.

1	bunch kale	1
1 tbsp	sesame oil	15 mL
1 cup	sliced cremini mushrooms	250 mL
2 tsp	soy OR tamari sauce	10 mL

1. Cut off stalks from the kale; wash. Boil for 5 minutes and then drain; chop into 2-inch (5 cm) wide strips.

2. In a large frying pan, heat the oil. Add the mushrooms and sauté for 3 to 5 minutes.

3. Add the chopped kale. Stir-fry only to reheat.

4. Sprinkle with the soy or tamari sauce and serve.

apini

Serves 4–6

I love serving interesting, different vegetables. It really makes my day when someone sits down at my table and asks "What the heck is this?" Rapini, a staple in most Italian households, will elicit that kind of response.

This is a very neglected vegetable with incredible flavour and a powerful nutritional punch.

1	large bunch rapini	1
1 tbsp	olive oil	15 mL
2	cloves garlic, minced	2

1. Boil the rapini for 4 minutes. Drain well.

2. Heat a large frying pan. Add the oil. Quickly sauté the garlic so that it doesn't burn. Burnt garlic tastes awful, sort of like haggis on a bad day. (Little cross-cultural reference.)

3. Add the rapini and sauté until coated in the garlic and oil. Serve. It's simple but great.

Beet and Pear Purée

Serves 6–8

I conducted a little survey and asked people if they liked beets, eggplant, and purple-tipped broccoli. Nine out of ten people had never tried any of these vegetables. Inadvertently, I had stumbled upon a major culinary discovery: people are afraid of purple vegetables. Somewhere along the evolutionary food chain, the colour purple (although a great book) struck a note of fear in mortals. I can't imagine why.

Personally, I love all the aforementioned culprits. Then again, I love lima beans, so maybe I'm not a good example of a normal food-chain eater. So for all you other purple-vegetable lovers, here's a different beet recipe. You'll need a food processor.

4	medium beets (approx. ½ lb)	4
1 cup	finely chopped onion	250 mL
2 tbsp	unsalted butter	25 mL
2	Anjou or Bartlett pears, peeled, cored, and chopped	2
1 tbsp	maple syrup	15 mL
¼ cup	apple cider vinegar	50 mL
½ tsp	salt	2 mL

1. Boil the beets until tender, approximately 20 to 40 minutes. Skin. Chop coarsely.

2. In a large frying pan, sauté the onion in the butter for 10 minutes.

3. Add the pears, maple syrup, apple cider vinegar, and salt and sauté for 10 more minutes.

4. Pour the onion mixture into a food processor and pulse four times.

5. Add half the beets and pulse three times.

6. Add the remaining beets and pulse three more times. The beet mixture should look chunky—like a "big" relish.

7. Serve, or refrigerate until 10 minutes before serving time and reheat.

wiss Chard

Serves 4–6

Swiss chard is a member of the beet family. Any beet lover worth his or her salt knows that beet tops are the best part of the beet. So it should come as no surprise that the leafy green Swiss chard is one outstanding vegetable.

I cook beet tops and Swiss chard the same way. (I just called the recipe *Swiss Chard* hoping to get your attention. I figured you'd read *Beet Tops* and be flipping to the next page.)

| 1 | bunch Swiss chard OR beet tops, cleaned | 1 |
| 1 tbsp | balsamic or rice vinegar | 15 mL |

1. Wash the Swiss chard or beet tops and steam for 5 to 6 minutes.

2. Drain well. Chop into 3-inch (8 cm) wide pieces.

3. Sprinkle the balsamic or rice vinegar on top. Serve.

Carrots

Vegetable Side Dishes

Serves 4–6

"Eat your carrots, they're good for you." I've heard that a million times. As a kid, I disliked cooked carrots but couldn't figure out why. As an adult, I know why: overcooked carrots don't taste good. Okay, it's not a revolutionary answer—but it is true. So add a little butter, a little honey, and a little mustard. Here's the recipe—and don't overcook them.

2 lb	baby carrots	1 kg
1 tbsp	butter	15 mL
1 tbsp	liquid honey	15 mL
1 tsp	Dijon mustard	5 mL

1. Clean the baby carrots. (I said *clean*, not *peel*. It's that fibre–flavour thing I like so much.)

2. In a medium-sized pot, boil the carrots for 5 to 8 minutes, depending on their size and your definition of tender-crisp.

3. While they are boiling, melt together the butter, honey, and mustard.

4. Drain the carrots. Save the water for stock or throw all those lovely nutrients down the drain . . . your choice.

5. Pour the butter mixture over the carrots. Toss and serve.

quash and Rutabaga Purée

Serves 8–10

So, you were going to skip this recipe, weren't you? Took one look at the title and were just about to flip to the dessert section. Well, are *you* in for a surprise.

You'll like this so much, you can serve it to your turnip-hating Uncle Martin. He'll never know he's eating the queen of the neglected root vegetables! Best part— he'll ask for seconds. Wait 'til he's finished before you tell him the truth . . .

1	medium rutabaga (approx. 1 lb/ 500 g)	1
1	medium butternut or buttercup squash (approx. 2 lb/ 1 kg)	1
2	medium onions, sliced	2
1 cup	chicken stock	250 mL
1 tbsp	butter (optional)	15 mL
	Salt and pepper	

1. Peel and chop the rutabaga.

2. Peel the squash, remove seeds, and chop the pulp.

3. Put the rutabaga, squash, and onion into a large saucepan.

4. Add the chicken stock. Bring to a boil, cover, and reduce heat. Simmer for 20 to 30 minutes or until vegetables are tender.

5. Drain well. Reserve liquid for soup stock or gravy, or store in the back of the fridge for three weeks before discarding.

6. Purée vegetables. Add butter, if using. Add salt and pepper to taste. Serve immediately or refrigerate for up to four days.

O ven-Fried Mushrooms

Serves 2 mushroom lovers or 4 normal people

You should never bump a cooking mushroom or wake a sleeping baby. The lesson is leave well enough alone. This is the easiest recipe in the book, and it makes a great-tasting treat.

Somewhere along the cooking chain, people began to think that the more steps there were in a recipe, the better the result. Well, "It ain't necessarily so."

| 1 lb | medium button mushrooms | 500 g |
| 1 tbsp | olive oil | 15 mL |

1. Preheat oven to 375°F (190°C).

2. Into an oven-tempered pan or a cast-iron frying pan—which is what I use—pour the oil.

3. Add the mushrooms and stir until they are coated with oil.

4. Roast in the oven for 20 minutes. Then, and only then, stir them gently.

5. Roast for 15 more minutes. Serve.

Scalloped Potatoes

Serves 4–6

Scalloped potatoes are fattening. Some things lend themselves to becoming fat reduced—scalloped potatoes don't. If anything, they beg for *more* fat. So if your arteries are up for it, use 35% whipping cream instead of homogenized milk.

4	large baking potatoes, peeled and cut in ¼-inch (5 mm) slices	4
Pinch	salt	Pinch
4	large onions, thinly sliced	4
4	cloves garlic, minced	4
¼ cup	butter	50 mL
2 cups	homogenized milk	500 mL
2 tbsp	all-purpose flour	25 mL
	Salt and pepper	

1. Put the sliced potatoes into a large pot. Barely cover with water. Lightly salt the water and boil, covered, for 15 minutes or until potatoes are fairly tender. Don't overboil—you want the slices to retain their shape.

2. Meanwhile, in a large frying pan, sauté the onions and garlic in the butter until the onions are translucent.

3. Preheat oven to 350°F (180°C).

4. Heat the milk until steamy.

5. Grease a 9-inch (2.5 L) square baking dish.

6. Line the pan with a piece of parchment paper that completely covers the bottom and sides of the pan. This step is optional but it does help in the awful cleaning-up part.

7. When the potatoes are done, drain well.

8. Begin the layering process. Layer half the potatoes, sprinkle 1 tablespoon (15 mL) of the flour, and then spoon in half the onion mixture. Repeat, topping with the onion mixture. Add salt and pepper to taste.

9. Pour the hot milk over top. Bake, uncovered, for 35 to 40 minutes.

10. When the potatoes are golden brown, sit and rest for 10 minutes. You *and* the potatoes.

ashed Potatoes

Serves 4–8

I know everyone knows how to make mashed potatoes. Mine, however, are just a little different. Check them out.

4	large russet potatoes, preferably P.E.I.	4
3	cloves garlic	3
Pinch	salt	Pinch
3 tbsp	butter	45 mL
3 tbsp	35% whipping cream or whole milk	45 mL
	Salt and pepper	

1. Peel and quarter the potatoes. Barely cover with water and add the secret ingredient—garlic. Lightly salt the water.

2. Boil, covered, until the potatoes are cooked but not mushy. They should still look like potatoes cut into quarters. The cooking time will vary between 15 and 25 minutes, depending on the size of the potatoes. Just keep checking.

3. Just before the spuds are ready, heat the butter and cream or milk until the butter is melted. Cream makes the potatoes taste creamier. Big surprise.

4. Drain the potatoes. Now mash. Really mash the heck out of them. Get rid of all your frustrations and really give it to those potatoes.

5. Pour in the butter mixture and mash again. Add salt and pepper to taste.

> **Pitfall** Normally this dish will serve eight, but it's so good it will probably feed only four. I can eat half the pot myself. (And I wonder why I can't lose weight?)

ven-Roasted Fries

Serves me, or 4 regular people

I love fries, but I don't like all that fat. So I created my version of oven-roasted fries. The less fattening, less messy, way longer method. It's worth the hour it takes to cook them. (Patience is a virtue—one I really need to cultivate.)

4	large baking potatoes, preferably P.E.I.	4
2 tbsp	olive oil	25 mL
½ tsp	seasoned salt	2 mL
½ tsp	pepper	2 mL
½ tsp	garlic powder	2 mL
1 tsp	paprika	5 mL

1. Preheat the oven to 375°F (190°C).

2. Scrub the potatoes. We're not peeling them. Extra fibre and flavour.

3. Cut into fries about 1-inch (2.5 cm) thick.

4. Put the fries into a large bowl. Pour the olive oil over them and toss to coat them. Sprinkle on the salt, pepper, garlic powder, and paprika. Toss again.

5. Dump the fries onto a baking sheet that you've lined with parchment paper because you know the pan will be a snap to wash up later. Spread the fries out evenly.

6. Bake for 30 minutes. Take them out and turn them so they will be golden brown all over.

7. Put them back in the oven for 20 to 30 minutes longer.

Pitfall #1 You cut the potatoes so small that they are crispy, burnt things. Tell everyone they are potato chip fries. Next time, follow step 3.

Pitfall #2 They are soggy. You piled them on top of each other. Reread step 5. Spread them out and put them back in the oven for 15 more minutes.

Note For really low-fat fries, omit olive oil and dump the fries onto parchment paper. Sprinkle with salt, pepper, garlic powder, and paprika. Then follow step 6.

Yams

Serves 4–6

All cooks have their little culinary secrets. One of mine is frozen orange juice concentrate. I use it as a flavouring for lots of different dishes. Its intense flavour goes well with plain yogurt poured over fresh strawberries or makes an interesting addition to plain old cream cheese icing.

I particularly like it mixed with yams. The flavour is wonderful and you don't even need to add the fat culprit—butter.

2	large yams	2
	(approx. 1 lb / 500 g)	
3–4 tbsp	frozen orange juice concentrate, thawed	45–60 mL

1. Preheat oven to 350°F (180°C).

2. Scrub the yams and prick them with a fork.

3. Bake for 1 to 1½ hours or until soft. Or run out and buy a microwave! Then cook for only 10 to 12 minutes on High.

4. Once they are soft, let them rest in a bowl for 5 minutes.

5. This little "yam pick-me-up" makes it easy to skin them, which just happens to be the next step. Skin yams.

6. Mash the yams together with 3 tablespoons (45 mL) of the orange juice concentrate.

7. For a more intense orange flavour, add 1 more tablespoon (15 mL) of concentrate.

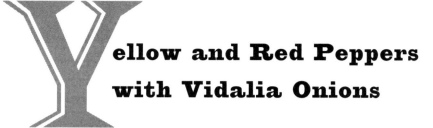

Yellow and Red Peppers with Vidalia Onions

Serves 4–6

Vidalia onions are sweet and juicy and are usually available from May to the end of June. They go wonderfully with sweet yellow and red peppers.

1 ½ tbsp	olive oil	22 mL
1	large Vidalia onion, thinly sliced	1
2	medium sweet yellow peppers, thinly sliced	2
2	medium sweet red peppers, thinly sliced	2
1 tbsp	balsamic vinegar	15 mL

1. Heat a large frying pan. Add the olive oil.

2. Add the onion and sauté until almost translucent, 4 to 5 minutes.

3. Add the yellow and red pepper strips and sauté for 2 more minutes or until hot and tender-crisp.

4. Add the balsamic vinegar and sauté for 30 seconds. Serve.

Roasted Veggie Packets

Serves 4

Ever get a hankerin' for a barbecue in the middle of winter? Too cold to go outside? Wrap up some veggies in foil and pop them into the oven. If you don't seal the foil correctly, your oven could catch fire and then it would even *feel* like barbecue season!

16	new red potatoes, scrubbed	16
12	baby carrots, cleaned	12
12	pearl onions, peeled	12
4 tbsp	butter	60 mL
4	cloves garlic	4
	Salt and pepper	

1. Preheat oven to 400°F (200°C).

2. Parboil the potatoes, carrots, and onions for 5 to 7 minutes. To parboil means to partially cook. The potatoes, carrots, and onions need to boil for several minutes so they won't take forever to roast in the oven. It's a cooking shortcut!

3. Take four pieces of tin foil, each about 10 inches (25 cm) long. Lay out on the counter.

4. Drain the vegetables. Divide them equally between the four pieces of foil.

5. Put 1 tablespoon (15 mL) of the butter on top of each portion. Press the garlic into the melting butter. Add salt and pepper to taste.

6. Wrap up packages: bring the four corners up to the centre and seal. (To prevent fires, really seal the packages. As a further precaution, bake on a jelly roll pan.)

7. Bake for 25 minutes.

Rice and Other Grains

Rice has been cultivated for five millennia. It comes in white, brown, purple, and red, and as short grain, long grain, quick cooking, and other forms. All in all, rice is a very eclectic little grain.

Rice Ranking

1. Brown rice is a highly nutritious complex carbohydrate that has all of its nutrients intact. It is by far my first choice for flavour and nutrition. Rank #1.

2. Wild rice isn't rice at all. It's a long-grain marsh grass. It doesn't really belong here, but I'd give it a rank #1½.

3. Converted or parboiled rice is white rice that, through a pressure-steaming method, has had some if its nutrients forced into the kernel. Rank #2.

4. White rice has had the majority of its nutrients scraped off, hence the name it sometimes goes by—polished rice. Rank #3.

5. Basmati, jasmine, and other aromatic rices tie in at rank #3.

6. Instant or quick rice—you should just forget about it.

Short Grain vs. Long Grain

In its cooked form, short-grain rice is stickier than long-grain rice. Short-grain rice is also denser. So, depending on your likes and dislikes, go with long grain if you want fluffy, separate rice kernels and short grain if you want sticky rice.

Rice Rules

1. Use a heavy pot with a tight-fitting lid.
2. Follow the "no peeking rule." Don't lift the lid to check on it. Simply watch the time. If you have been *simmering* it for the required length of time, it will be cooked. So don't peek.
3. If you don't peek, then you couldn't possibly be wrecking the rice by stirring it while it's cooking.
4. Never *ever* substitute white rice for brown. Brown rice absorbs more liquid than white. If you substitute willy-nilly, you will have watery, yucky, awful, soupy rice. Point made?
5. Eat brown rice. It's by far the healthiest choice. Your colon will thank you.

Rice and Other Grains

Dad's Rice Pilaf

Serves 4–8

My parents were visiting while I was testing recipes for this book. Timing is everything, don't you think? My father was on a low-cholesterol diet so I created some dishes especially for him. This is one of them.

2 cups	chicken stock	500 mL
1	medium onion, coarsely chopped	1
2	cloves garlic, minced	2
1 cup	long-grain brown rice	250 mL
	Salt and pepper	
2 tbsp	chopped fresh parsley	25 mL
2 tbsp	chopped fresh chives (optional)	25 mL

1. In a medium-sized pot, mix the chicken stock, onion, garlic, brown rice, and salt and pepper.

2. Bring to a boil. Cover and reduce heat. Simmer for 45 minutes or until the rice is tender.

3. Add the parsley and chives, if using. Toss with a fork and serve. (Recipes should all be this easy!)

Rice Pilaf with Toasted Hazelnuts

Serves 4–8

Here's one with fat. Lots of fat. Unfortunately, it has lots of flavour too. Why is it that fattening stuff tastes so good?

¼ cup	unsalted butter	50 mL
1	medium onion, chopped	1
1 cup	sliced mushrooms	250 mL
1½ cups	short-grain brown rice	375 mL
3 cups	chicken stock	750 mL
1 cup	hazelnuts, coarsely chopped	250 mL

Tip *The highly nutritious brown rice almost makes up for the fat. Eat only a small amount. Or, to lower the fat content, you could substitute 2 tablespoons (25 mL) olive oil for the ¼ cup (50 mL) unsalted butter. To lower it further, make Dad's Rice Pilaf (page 67) instead.*

1. In a heavy saucepan, melt the butter. Toss in the onion and sauté for 2 minutes or until translucent.

2. Add the mushrooms and cook for 5 minutes. Don't stir too often—you want the mushrooms to brown, not boil, in their own juices.

3. Add the rice and stir to coat.

4. Pour in the stock. Bring to a boil. Cover, reduce heat to simmer, and cook for 40 to 45 minutes or until the rice is tender.

5. Meanwhile, toast the hazelnuts. Here's a quickie version: heat a frying pan, add the hazelnuts, and stir until you see the skins popping off. Remove from heat. Stir, making sure none of them burn. Put them on a paper towel to cool. Rub the paper towel over them to remove the skins. When cool, chop coarsely.

6. Add the hazelnuts to the cooked rice and lightly stir until incorporated. Serve. Enjoy.

Livestock Purchases Record

Year _____

Date	No.	Type	Wt.	Price/lb	Total $	Seller
Carrot calves; Look Page 178						
" " You Can Count On 181						

Year _____

Deaths	Sales	Wt.	Tsf In	Tsf Out	Dec 31

- Deaths - Sales - Transfers Out = Dec 31

air's House Pilaf

Serves 4–6

I've been making this dish since my university days. Convincing my parents to try it was another matter. They finally had some this year and they loved it. My mom even asked me why I'd never served it before. Sometimes you just can't win.

1 tbsp	olive oil	15 mL
1 tbsp	butter	15 mL
1	medium onion, coarsely chopped	1
1 cup	long-grain brown rice	250 mL
1 tsp	turmeric	5 mL
½ tsp	curry powder	2 mL
½ tsp	allspice	2 mL
2 cups	chicken stock	500 mL
½ cup	chopped almonds (optional)	125 mL

1. In a medium-sized pot, heat the olive oil and butter. Toss in the onion and sauté for 2 minutes or until translucent.

2. Add the rice and stir to coat.

3. Add the spices—turmeric, curry powder, and allspice. Cook for 1 minute.

4. Add the chicken stock. Bring to a boil. Cover and reduce heat. Simmer for 50 minutes.

5. Fluff with a fork. Remove from heat and let sit for 5 minutes. Sprinkle with almonds, if using, and serve.

Curried Rice with Fresh Cilantro

Serves 4–6

This is a sticky, mild curry rice dish. It goes well with chicken and I find it's a nice and easy introduction to curry.

2 cups	chicken stock	500 mL
1 cup	short-grain brown rice	250 mL
1	medium onion, coarsely chopped	1
1 tsp	curry powder	5 mL
2 tbsp	chopped fresh cilantro	25 mL

1. In a medium-sized pot, stir together the chicken stock, rice, onion, and curry powder.

2. Bring to a boil. Cover and reduce to simmer. Cook for 45 minutes.

3. When done, fluff with a fork. Toss in cilantro and serve.

ice with Green Onions and Peas

Serves 4–8

A family-style, kid-approved rice. No weird spices, funny colours, or surprise tastes. What you see is what you get: converted rice, green onions, and peas!

If bungee jumping is not your cup of tea, you'll love this rice.

1 cup	converted rice	250 mL
2 cups	water	500 mL
¼ tsp	salt	1 mL
1 tbsp	butter	15 mL
½ cup	chopped green onions	125 mL
1 cup	peas, frozen are fine, thawed	250 mL

1. In a medium-sized pot, add the rice, water, and salt.

2. Bring to a boil. Cover and reduce heat to simmer for 25 minutes.

3. When cooked, remove from heat. Fluff with a fork and cover.

4. In a frying pan or skillet, melt the butter. Toss in the green onions and sauté for approximately 1 minute. Add the thawed peas. Heat through.

5. Add to the rice. Toss and cover. Let sit for 5 minutes; serve.

 Tip To thaw frozen peas, rinse under hot water; this takes all of 1 minute.

 **ild and Brown Rice**

Serves 4–6

Because wild rice is expensive, I buy small amounts and cook it with long-grain brown rice.

¼ cup	wild rice	50 mL
¾ cup	long-grain brown rice	175 mL
2 cups	chicken stock	500 mL

 Serving Suggestion
• *Poached Salmon (page 105)*

1. In a heavy pot, mix the wild rice, brown rice, and stock. Let sit for 2 hours.

2. Bring to a boil. Cover and reduce heat to simmer; cook for 55 to 60 minutes or until the liquid has been absorbed.

3. Fluff with a fork. Remove from heat and let sit for 10 minutes. Serve.

ouscous—Three Ways

Couscous? What on earth is it? you ask. Well, it's a nifty, granular cereal that has a nutty flavour and is ready in about 10 minutes. I like it as an alternative to rice, pasta, or potatoes, and I especially like it because it's so quick to fix. Serve it with fish—another quickie! I'm including three of my couscous recipes. Enjoy.

Plain Couscous

Serves 4–6

2 tbsp	butter	25 mL
1	shallot, minced	1
1 cup	couscous	250 mL
1½ cups	chicken stock	375 mL

1. In a medium-sized pot, melt the butter. Toss in the shallot and sauté for 5 minutes or until translucent.

2. Add the couscous and stir to coat.

3. Add the chicken stock. Bring to a boil. Reduce to simmer.

4. Simmer for 2 minutes.

5. Cover. Remove from heat. Let sit for 5 minutes. Fluff it up with a fork and serve. (Lots of fluffing with a fork in this chapter, isn't there?)

Couscous and Tomato

Serves 4–6

Just too darn easy for words. (Throw out your instant rice.)

1 tbsp	olive oil	15 mL
1 cup	couscous	250 mL
2 cups	tomato juice	500 mL

1. In a medium-sized pot, heat the oil. Add the couscous. Stir to coat.

2. Pour in the tomato juice. Bring to a boil. Reduce to simmer.

3. Simmer for 2 minutes.

4. Cover and remove from heat. Let sit for 5 minutes. Fluff it up with a fork and serve.

Couscous Pilaf

Serves 4–6

1 tbsp	butter	15 mL
1	medium onion, diced	1
1 cup	sliced mushrooms	250 mL
1 cup	couscous	250 mL
2 cups	chicken stock	500 mL

1. In a medium-sized pot, melt the butter. Toss in the onion and sauté for 2 minutes or until translucent.

2. Add the mushrooms. Cook until the mushrooms brown. Don't stir too often. Once or twice is fine.

3. Add the couscous and stir to coat.

4. Add the chicken stock. Bring to a boil. Reduce to simmer.

5. Simmer for 2 minutes.

6. Cover and remove from heat. Let sit for 7 minutes. Fluff up with a fork. Cover for 3 minutes; serve.

ulgur Pilaf

Serves 4–8

"She's doing it again! What's bulgur? I bet it's weird! Get out the dictionary."

Let me save you the trouble. Bulgur is wheat kernels that have been steamed, dried, and then cracked. It is a chewy, nutty-flavoured kernel that is a nice change from rice.

1 tbsp	olive oil	15 mL
1 tbsp	butter	15 mL
2	shallots, minced	2
½	Vidalia onion, diced	½
10	cremini or brown mushrooms, quartered	10
1 cup	bulgur	250 mL
2 cups	chicken stock	500 mL
Pinch	white pepper	Pinch

Note If you can't find Vidalia onions, substitute a Walla Walla or Spanish onion.

1. In a medium-sized pot, heat the oil and butter. Toss in the shallots and onion and sauté for 5 minutes or until translucent.

2. Add the mushrooms. You want to brown them to fully develop the flavours. Mix occasionally so they will not burn, but too much stirring makes them lose their liquid. You'll end up stewing them. Just brown them.

3. When they are browned, after approximately 5 minutes, add the bulgur and stir until well coated.

4. Add the chicken stock. Stir. Add the pepper. Stir.

5. Bring to a boil. Cover and reduce heat. Simmer for 20 minutes.

6. Fluff with a fork. Cover and let sit for 5 more minutes. Serve.

Pasta

When I was 12, I saw a movie called *Houseboat*, starring Cary Grant and Sophia Loren. Well, I'd always wondered why I didn't have any boyfriends. As I sat in the theatre watching Cary pursue Sophia, it dawned on me. Boobs. It all came down to boobs, and I didn't have any yet.

I began researching Sophia Loren. She had the best ones my 12-year-old eyes had ever seen. What was her secret? I read every magazine article I could find on her. Nowhere did she spell out the secret to her success. The only recurring theme was pasta. Sophia ate a lot of pasta. It must be the pasta, I surmised.

In those days, pasta was spaghetti that came out of a can. Despite its weird orange tinge, I began eating tons of it and checking the mirror every day to see if the miracle formula was working. I kept thinking . . . Sophia likes this stuff?

By Day 3, I thought I noticed a change in my upper torso. On closer examination, it appeared that my boobs were shrinking! Maybe I'd end up in the side show at the circus, "Ladies and gentlemen, step right up to see Meemee (my stage name) and her incredible shrinking bazooms." My life was over. Panic-stricken, I checked myself out once more. It wasn't my chest that was changing, it was . . . my belly! My gut was huge. Perhaps the pasta had lost the map to my mammary glands.

I decided I'd give it one more day. Stoically I swallowed another meal of "spaghetti in a can." I stripped down to my underwear and began the exam—I looked more like the Goodyear blimp than my beloved Sophia. After four gruelling days, I packed it in.

Fast forward to my twenties. I discovered the real world of pasta. Fettucine, linguine, rotini—the list is endless. Oh! I get it—this is why Sophia ate a lot of pasta.

Well, I've been eating Sophia's pasta for the past 20 years, and you know—I think it's finally working!

Pasta Rules

1. Use a big pot and lots of water. Pasta should be able to move around in the pot while cooking.

2. I say, "Salt!" Adding salt speeds up the cooking process because salty water has a higher boiling point; therefore the pasta will cook at a higher temperature. And the salt does add some flavour.

3. As soon as the pasta hits the water, give it a stir to help keep it from sticking.
4. Don't add oil to the water. You are just adding fat to a low-fat food and making the pasta slippery. Instead, use a bigger pot and more water.
5. When pasta is cooked it should be "al dente." In English, this term means "to the tooth." So pasta shouldn't be mushy; it should have some body without being chewy. Fresh pasta takes 3 to 4 minutes to reach the al dente stage; dried pasta, 6 to 7 minutes.

6. Drain pasta well but never rinse it. Rinsing is a bad thing because (1) there go some nutrients down the drain and (2) sauce won't stick to rinsed pasta.

Pasta

airlyn's Spicy, Blow-Your-Head-Off Pasta

Serves 4–6

Oprah had a cooking contest back in 1995. She had all these categories: Fish, Chicken, Ethnic, Quick, Low-fat, and so on. Well, I love Oprah, so I decided to wow her with three categories in one— Ethnic, Quick, and Low-Fat.

I videotaped my son and me coming in the back door saying we'd just finished playing hockey on our frozen pond in the backyard and wow was it ever cold in September here in Canada! Andrew helped me cook and he wore his hockey helmet the whole time. We thought we were hysterical.

I sent off our video with this recipe and patiently waited for Oprah to call. I was sure I'd win something. I'm still waiting. Maybe she lost my number?

1 tbsp	balsamic vinegar	15 mL
2	medium onions, diced	2
1	bag spinach, washed and chopped	1
1	can (28 oz/796 mL) plum tomatoes, drained and chopped	1
10	sun-dried tomatoes (not in oil), chopped	10
6	spicy black olives, pitted and chopped	6
2	cloves garlic, minced	2
6 oz	marinated artichokes, drained well	170 mL
1–2 tsp	red pepper flakes	5–10 mL
1 tbsp	pesto	15 mL
1	package (4 cups/350 g) fresh spinach rigatoni	1

1. Put the water on to boil for the pasta.

2. Heat a large non-stick pan. Add the balsamic vinegar and onions. Stir.

3. Add the spinach. Stir; simmer, covered, for 2 minutes.

4. Add the tomatoes—canned and sundried. Cover. Simmer for 2 minutes.

5. Add the olives, garlic, and artichokes. Now the red pepper flakes—these are really hot. Add 1 teaspoon (5 mL) first and taste. If you want the sauce to be spicier, add another teaspoon (5 mL) and mix well. Cover pan and simmer.

6. Boil pasta for 3 to 4 minutes. Drain.

7. Add pesto to sauce. Stir. Dump over top of the pasta. Toss and serve.

Two-Cheese Ravioli

**Serves 4 as an appetizer,
2 as an entrée**

Most people think they hate foods they've never actually tried.

I regularly fib. That is, I don't tell people exactly what they are eating until after they've eaten it.

Mairlyn: Here, try this.
Friend: What is it?
Mairlyn: Do you have any allergies?
Friend: No . . .
Mairlyn: It's fabulous. Just try . . . No dessert unless you do.
Friend: [Munch, munch, munch.] This is fabulous.
Mairlyn: Best eye of newt I've ever made.

My Two-Cheese Ravioli has Gorgonzola and feta cheese in it. It's a wonderful combo of flavours. So, for all those "I know I hate blue cheese" folks, just give it a try.

Filling

½ cup	minced onion	125 mL
1	shallot, minced	1
1 tbsp	olive oil	15 mL
2 tbsp	pine nuts	25 mL
1½ oz	feta cheese, crumbled	40 g
	(approx. ⅓ cup/75 mL)	
1½ oz	Gorgonzola cheese,	40 g
	crumbled	
	(approx. ⅓ cup/75 mL)	

Pesto

1	jar (11 oz/314 mL)	1
	roasted red peppers	
	OR 8 large sweet red	
	peppers, roasted	
1 cup	fresh parsley	250 mL
3	cloves garlic	3
1 tbsp	lemon juice	15 mL

Pasta

24	square won ton wrappers	24

1. Heat water in a large pasta pot or stockpot. Bring to a boil.

2. While that happens, make the filling. In a frying pan, sauté the onions and shallots in the olive oil.

3. When tender, add the pine nuts. Cook for 2 minutes, stirring constantly. Remove from heat.

4. In a medium-sized bowl, mix the two cheeses. Add the onion mixture and stir. The heat will slightly melt the cheese. Set aside.

5. Make the pesto. Either by hand or using a food processor, finely chop and mix the roasted red peppers, parsley, and garlic. Don't pulverize. The peppers should still be recognizable. Put into a saucepan; add the lemon juice and heat. Don't cook it—just heat it.

6. Make the ravioli. Lay out twelve won ton wrappers in rows of three. Spoon 1 to 2 teaspoons (5–10 mL) of the filling in the centre of six wrappers. Put a little water on the edges and lay top piece on. Seal. Then press with a fork to make sure they are firmly sealed.

7. Make six more, for a total of twelve ravioli.

8. Slide ravioli into gently boiling water. Cook for 2 to 4 minutes. Overcooking makes the ravioli fall apart.

9. Remove from water with a slotted spoon and place on a clean tea towel to remove excess water.

10. Serve with pesto sauce spooned over.

Plain-and-Simple Plum Tomato Sauce

Serves 4

This is my house sauce recipe. In August and September, when my local greengrocer sells plum tomatoes by the bushel, I make this two or three times a week. I even freeze the tomatoes whole for a fresh-tasting sauce in December. When I run out of frozen ones, I use canned. Fresh, frozen, canned—three choices for the same great sauce.

10	fresh (or frozen) plum tomatoes, skinned,* OR 1 (28 oz/796 mL) can plum tomatoes, drained	10
4	cloves garlic, mashed	4
1 tbsp	Worcestershire sauce	15 mL
2 tbsp	chopped fresh basil OR 1 tbsp (15 mL) dried	25 mL
4 cups	dried penne	1 L
	Freshly grated Parmesan cheese (optional)	

1. I use a cast-iron frying pan. The acid from the tomatoes helps absorb iron from the pan. So, in a cast-iron frying pan, simmer the tomatoes, garlic, and Worcestershire. Crush the tomatoes with a fork or a potato masher.

2. Simmer the sauce for 40 minutes. Just before serving, add the basil.

3. Put the water on to boil. Cook pasta 6 to 7 minutes. Drain.

4. Pour the sauce over the cooked pasta. Sprinkle with the Parmesan, if using.

> ✳ *How to skin a tomato (or is it peel)? I call it **skinning** because I pour boiling water over top of them. The skins come off easily. **Peeling** to me means you use a peeler. So my book, my rules: it's called **skinning**.*

Shells with Italian Chili Sauce

Serves 12, or 6 with leftovers

This recipe makes a ton! It makes a lot on purpose. My life is very hectic and even I need a break from cooking dinner every night. If I know I'm going to have a busy week, I'll make this on a Monday night, and then we'll have it again on Wednesday. On Monday I'll serve it with broccoli and carrots. On Wednesday I'll broil some cheese on top and serve it with fresh Italian bread and a salad.

This is my son's favourite pasta dish. He loves it with broccoli. It just goes to show that if you serve this kind of meal to two-year-olds, they'll pick it as their favourite when they're seven!

1 tbsp	olive oil	15 mL
1	medium onion, diced	1
½ lb	ground turkey or chicken	250 g
4	cloves garlic, chopped	4
1	can (28 oz/796 mL) plum tomatoes, drained	1
1	can (19 oz/540 mL) kidney beans, drained	1
1	can (5½ oz/156 mL) tomato paste	1
2 tbsp	chopped fresh basil OR 1 tbsp (15 mL) dried	25 mL
1 tsp	dried oregano	5 mL
1 tbsp	Worcestershire sauce	15 mL
1 tbsp	balsamic vinegar	15 mL
1	package (1 lb/450 g) shell pasta	1
	Grated mozzarella or Cheddar cheese (optional)	

1. In a large saucepan, heat the oil. Toss in the onion and sauté for 2 minutes or until translucent.

2. Add the ground turkey or chicken and cook for 6 minutes or until all the pink is gone.

3. Add the garlic, plum tomatoes, kidney beans, tomato paste, basil, oregano, Worcestershire, and balsamic vinegar.

4. Simmer for 40 minutes.

5. Put the water on to boil. Cook fresh pasta for 3 to 4 minutes. (Dried pasta takes 6 to 7 minutes.) Drain.

6. Add the cooked pasta to the sauce. Stir to mix.

7. Serve with mozzarella or Cheddar sprinkled on top, if using.

8. Store any leftovers in the fridge for up to 3 days.

resh Spinach Pasta with Bocconcini and Rapini

Serves 4

Bocconcini are bite-sized rounds of fresh mozzarella. You can find it in cheese shops, in specialty grocery stores, or in a well-stocked supermarket in the cheese section. It is a fresh cheese so it doesn't last long—check the best-before date.

This pasta dish is spicy, colourful, and quick to make. I like to serve it with spinach fettucine, fresh preferably, but dried is good too.

1	Package (⅔ lb/350 g) fresh spinach fettucine	1
1	bunch rapini	1
1 tbsp	olive oil	15 mL
3	cloves garlic, minced	3
½ cup	sun-dried tomatoes in oil, drained and chopped	125 mL
12	black olives, pitted and halved	12
1 tsp	red pepper flakes	5 mL
8	slices bocconcini, cut into small pieces	8

1. Put water on to boil for the pasta. Add the pasta and cook for 3 to 4 minutes. Drain.

2. Meanwhile, in a separate pot, boil the rapini for 5 minutes. Drain and chop.

3. In a large non-stick pan, heat the olive oil. Sauté the rapini and garlic, making sure not to burn the garlic.

4. Add the tomatoes, black olives, and red pepper flakes. Heat through.

5. Dish out the pasta onto four plates. Spoon the rapini mixture over top.

6. Divide the bocconcini between the four plates. Toss. Serve. Explain to everyone what the little white balls are. Use your imagination.

Rotini with Feta and Tomatoes

Serves 4

A non-cooked sauce. While the pasta is boiling, chop up the tomatoes, crumble the feta, halve the olives, and open the vino.

4 cups	dried rotini	1 L
1	large beefsteak tomato, chopped into 12–16 pieces	1
8	spicy black olives, pitted and halved	8
4 oz	feta, crumbled finely	113 g
2 tbsp	balsamic vinegar	25 mL
½ cup	chopped fresh chives	125 mL
	Freshly cracked pepper	

1. Put water on to boil. Add the rotini and cook for 6 to 7 minutes or until tender.

2. Combine the tomato, olives, feta, vinegar, and chives.

3. When pasta is cooked, drain, and return to pot.

4. Add the ingredients you assembled in step 2. Toss. Crack on some pepper and serve.

cott's Pasta, Only Better

Serves 4

My partner in crime, Scott, invented this dish. He boils pasta, drains it, and pours salad dressing on top. He has endless varieties and is limited only to what his grocer stocks.

Aside from the fact that Scott's recipe makes an extremely fattening entrée, it is a great idea. So, I've adapted his idea to fit a lower-fat, healthier version.

This recipe is great for one of those nights that all three of your kids have to be at different hockey rinks at the same time and your partner is out of town.

 Tip *To thaw frozen peas, rinse under hot water; this takes all of 1 minute.*

4 cups	dried rotini, shells, or penne	1 L
1	can (6.5 oz/ 184 g) water-packed tuna, drained and chopped	1
1 cup	frozen peas, thawed	250 mL
½ cup	chopped fresh chives	125 mL
¾ cup	low-calorie ranch dressing	175 mL
1	large sweet red pepper, chopped	1
	Salt and pepper	

1. Put the water on to boil. Add the pasta and cook for 6 to 7 minutes or until tender.

2. Combine the tuna, peas, chives, ranch dressing, and red pepper.

3. When pasta is cooked, drain, and return to pot.

4. Add the combined ingredients; toss. Add salt and pepper to taste.

5. Serve. Eat quickly and rush out the door.

ettucine with Smoked Salmon and Peas

Serves 6–8

This dish is fat laden and extremely delicious. It's an elegant pasta dish that's so good it can be served to your boss. As long as he or she isn't counting calories or cholesterol, you may even get a raise.

 Tip *To thaw frozen peas, rinse under hot water; this takes all of 1 minute.*

1	package (⅔ lb/ 350 g) fresh spinach fettucine	1
1	large onion, diced	1
2	cloves garlic, minced	2
2 tbsp	butter	25 mL
½ tsp	white pepper	2 mL
¼ tsp	salt	1 mL
2 cups	whipping cream or half-and-half	500 mL
6 oz	smoked salmon, chopped	170 g
1 cup	peas, fresh or frozen	250 mL

1. Put water on for pasta.

2. In a medium-sized pot, sauté the onion and garlic in the butter until soft.

3. Add the pepper and salt.

4. Add the cream. Bring to a gentle boil and cook for 3 minutes.

5. While that's boiling, cook the pasta.

6. After the 3 minutes, add the salmon to the cream mixture. Reduce the heat to simmer. Add the peas.

7. Drain the pasta. Put it back in the pot. Pour the cream sauce over the pasta. Toss and serve.

Poultry

"Handle raw poultry carefully or basically you'll die." I say that on "Harrowsmith Country Living" all the time. I'm kidding—but not altogether. Any raw meat that you handle needs to be treated according to my handy dandy rules:

Poultry Rules

1. Keep it in the fridge.
2. Marinate it in the fridge.
3. Keep it in the fridge.
4. Wash hands well before and after handling.
5. Keep it in the fridge.
6. Scrub your working surface with bleach if you've had raw meat on it.
7. Keep it in the fridge.
8. Thaw it in the fridge or in cold water.
9. Keep it in the fridge.

> **Note** I hope that my "keep it in the fridge" message was not overstated!

ornish Hens à l'Orange

Serves 4 (may be doubled)

I remember watching Graham Kerr, TV's Galloping Gourmet, flambé a chicken. I was 12 years old and very impressed that all his hair hadn't been burnt off his head. (I was still recovering from a bad Coleman stove experience.)

I knew that if Graham could do it so could I. Even back then, I had goals—okay, they were a little trite—but I did have goals. Today, I can flambé a chicken with the best of them. Two rules: heat the alcohol, turn off the stove, and then ignite; and always have a big lid or a fire extinguisher handy. You can never be too careful.

2	Cornish hens, split in half	2
	Salt and pepper	
3 tbsp	butter, softened	45 mL
2	oranges	2
¼ cup	orange brandy	50 mL
1 tbsp	all-purpose flour	15 mL
1 cup	chicken stock	250 mL

1. Preheat oven to 375°F (190°C).

2. In a shallow roasting pan, arrange the hens bone-side down. Sprinkle with the salt and pepper and dot with the butter.

3. The hens need to cook for 1½ hours. Baste and turn them frequently. They need to have golden to dark brown skin.

4. While the hens are cooking, zest the oranges and then pith and segment them (see Methods and Techniques, page 7). Reserve zest and segments.

5. When the hens are cooked, remove to a serving platter and keep warm. The hens are cooked when the juices run clear. (They will definitely be cooked in 1½ hours.)

6. Put the roasting pan on an element. Heat up. Pour in the orange brandy; heat slightly. Turn off the heat and ignite. (Don't use a butane lighter. A long-handled match is best.)

7. When the flames go out, stir in the flour. Stir constantly to make a paste. Turn the heat on and brown the paste.

8. Slowly add the chicken stock, whisking the whole time. Cook, whisking, until sauce thickens.

9. Add the orange segments and zest. Heat through.

10. Pour over hens and serve.

Serving Suggestions
- *Wild and Brown Rice (page 72)*
- *Asparagus with Lime Mayonnaise (page 20)*
- *Oven-Fried Mushrooms (page 57)*

ornish Hens with Cranberries
(and a whole lot of other stuff)

Serves 6 (don't double)

This is one of my favourite "let's impress the socks off the _____" (fill in the blank—I've used boss, neighbour, and ex-boyfriends). There may seem to be a lot of ingredients and steps to follow in the recipe, but it's fairly simple. Prepare part of the sauce beforehand so you can chat up the guests—then pop into the kitchen for ten minutes and return with this fabulous main course. It'll get oohs and aahs, and that's one of the main reasons we cook, isn't it?

3	Cornish hens, split in half	3

Jelly Mixture

½ cup	currant jelly	125 mL
⅓ cup	Cranraspberry Cocktail	75 mL
2 tbsp	Dijon mustard	25 mL

Spinach–Mushroom Mixture

2	bunches baby spinach	2
4	slices bacon	4
12	mushrooms, sliced	12
3 tbsp	olive oil	45 mL
3 tbsp	balsamic vinegar	45 mL
1 ½ tsp	water	7 mL
2 tsp	Dijon mustard	10 mL
1 ½ tsp	maple syrup	7 mL
	or liquid honey	
¼ tsp	salt	1 mL
½ cup	Cranraspberry Cocktail	125 mL
¼ cup	dried cranberries	50 mL

Garnish

8	slices red onion	8

1. Preheat oven to 400°F (200°C).

2. Mix together the currant jelly, Cran-raspberry Cocktail, and Dijon mustard.

3. Lay the hens bone-side down in a shallow roasting pan. Pour the jam mixture over the hens.

4. Roast for 25 minutes.

5. Turn hens over. Baste. Roast for 10 minutes.

6. Turn hens over again. Baste. Roast 10 more minutes; the skin will brown nicely. The hens are cooked when the juices run clear.

Meanwhile, or earlier in the day:

1. Wash and dry the spinach; set aside.

2. Fry the bacon until crisp. Lay bacon on paper towel and discard the grease. Reserve bacon.

3. Return the pan to the heat. (Don't wipe clean—you want the bacon flavour without all that grease.) Sauté the mushrooms; let brown in the pan.

4. While they're browning, mix together the olive oil, balsamic vinegar, water, Dijon mustard, maple syrup or honey, salt, Cranraspberry Cocktail, and cranberries.

5. Pour over the mushrooms and simmer for 3 minutes. (If you're making this ahead of time, cover and refrigerate. Then, 10 minutes before serving, reheat.)

Showtime!

6. Reheat the mushroom sauce—unless it's already hot!

7. Take out cooked hens.

8. Add the spinach to the hot mushroom sauce. Let wilt—just.

9. Spoon the spinach-mushroom mixture (save the sauce) onto a serving platter. Arrange hens on top, skin side up. Lay the red onion slices on top, and sprinkle with crumbled bacon. Pour the hot sauce over top. Serve. Humbly accept raves. Sit down and secretly gloat.

Serving Suggestions
- *Wild and Brown Rice (page 72)*
- *Brussels Sprouts (page 49)*

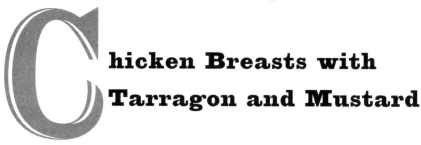

Chicken Breasts with Tarragon and Mustard

Serves 4 (may be doubled)

I planted some tarragon the first spring I moved into my house in Toronto. Eleven years later, I need a machete to harvest it. I had no idea that it would be so hardy, persistent, and fertile. Three excellent qualities in plants and animals.

I couldn't throw it out even though it threatened the health and safety of my peonies. After all, I'm the daughter of parents who lived through the Depression. I now make tarragon vinegar with it. *A lot* of tarragon vinegar. I also make this excellent chicken dish, which is easy to make and impressive to serve.

2 tbsp	olive oil	25 mL
4	large, boneless, skinless chicken breasts (approx. 1 lb/ 500 g)	4
1 tbsp	unsalted butter	15 mL
1 tbsp	olive oil	15 mL
½ cup	minced shallots	125 mL
3	cloves garlic, minced	3
½ cup	white wine, preferably chardonnay	125 mL
1 cup	chicken stock	250 mL
½ cup	whipping cream	125 mL
3 tbsp	grainy Dijon mustard	45 mL
2 tbsp	finely chopped fresh tarragon	25 mL
	Salt and pepper	

1. In a heavy skillet, heat 1 tablespoon (15 mL) of the olive oil. Add the chicken and cook until no longer pink on the inside. (I make sure they are brown on both sides.) Transfer to a holding dish; keep warm.

2. Back to the heavy skillet: add the butter and the remaining olive oil. Sauté the shallots and garlic; make sure not to burn the garlic.

3. Add the white wine and chicken stock. Crank up the heat and reduce the liquid until there is about ½ cup (125 mL) left, 3 to 5 minutes.

4. Reduce heat to medium low and whisk in the cream and mustard. Cook until it "thickens slightly." Okay—what does that mean? It means that, when you first add the cream, the mixture will be slightly watery looking. As you keep stirring over medium-low heat, it will thicken up. This takes between 2 and 5 minutes, depending on your stove.

5. When it has thickened slightly, put the chicken back in. Sprinkle with the tarragon. Put a lid on the skillet and reduce the heat to simmer. Add salt and pepper to taste, and serve.

Serving Suggestions
- *Mashed Potatoes (page 59)*
- *Yams (page 61)*

alsa-Broiled Chicken Breasts

Serves 4 (may be doubled)

Food has played an integral part in my life. Unlike most people, who can connect a special event in their lives to what they were wearing, what song was playing, or who they were with at that moment, I always remember what I was eating. Case in point:

1. First landing on the moon—brownies.
2. First date—poached salmon.
3. First divorce—Salsa-Broiled Chicken.

Hope you have better luck when you serve it.

1¼ cups	salsa, commercial brand, medium to hot (or see page 17)	300 mL
½ cup	Dijon mustard	125 mL
1 tbsp	lime juice	15 mL
2	cloves garlic, minced	2
4	boneless, skinless chicken breasts (approx. 1 lb/500 g)	4

1. In a large resealable plastic bag, mix together the salsa, Dijon mustard, lime juice, and garlic.

2. Add the chicken breasts. Seal the bag, squeezing air out as you go. Then swoosh the chicken around in the sauce. Stick it in the fridge to marinate for 4 hours.

3. Preheat the broiler. Pour the marinade into a pot. Bring to a boil. Cover and simmer for 10 minutes.

4. Meanwhile, broil the chicken breasts 3 or 4 inches away from the flame or element. Broil until golden brown on the first side, 6 to 8 minutes.

5. Turn chicken breasts. Spoon on lots of the cooked marinade. This side may take a little longer to cook, approximately 8 minutes. Chicken is cooked when meat is no longer pink inside. The salsa marinade should be almost black in spots and very bubbly.

6. Serve the chicken black side up. If there is any of the cooked marinade left over, serve on the side or on top of some rice.

Serving Suggestions
- Plain brown rice
- Dessert—Raspberry Sorbet (page 165) Family Brownies (page 146)

hicken, Hunter's Style

Serves 6

Hunter's style? What? Some hunter just happened to have a pot with garlic, peppers, stewed tomatoes, and wine in it? Okay, maybe the wine, but the other stuff? If anyone knows why they call this dish "Hunter's Style," write and tell me the reason.

6	boneless, skinless chicken breasts (approx. 1½ lb/750 g)	6
2 tbsp	olive oil	25 mL
2 tbsp	butter	25 mL
4	medium onions, quartered	4
2	large sweet red peppers, chopped	2
6	cloves garlic, minced	6
1 tsp	dried basil	5 mL
½ tsp	salt	2 mL
½ tsp	pepper	2 mL
1 cup	stewed tomatoes	250 mL
½ cup	dry red wine	125 mL
½ cup	tomato paste (optional)	125 mL

1. In a Dutch oven, brown the chicken breasts in the olive oil and butter. When just brown, remove and set aside.

2. Sauté the onions, red pepper, and garlic in the same pot. Add the basil, salt, pepper, and stewed tomatoes. Add the chicken. Bring to a boil. Cover, reduce heat, and simmer for 20 minutes.

3. Add the red wine and simmer for 10 minutes.

4. At this point, the sauce is very thin. What I like to do next is remove the chicken and vegetables. I then serve them with pasta and just spoon a little of the liquid on top (I use the remaining liquid as a soup stock for tomorrow's supper). Or I remove the chicken and vegetables, keep them hot, and add the tomato paste to the stock to thicken it. I reduce the sauce for 5 minutes to further thicken it and then serve over pasta. Your choice.

Serving Suggestions
- *With pasta*
- *Rapini (page 52)*
- *Carrots (page 55)*

urmeric Chicken

Serves 4 (may be doubled)

Turmeric's intense yellow-orange colour is what gives American-style prepared mustard its colour. If you happen to get any on your hands, it'll stain so well you'll look like you've been smoking for at least 60 years. Use the leftover lime to rub off the stain.

2 tsp	curry powder	10 mL
2 tsp	turmeric	10 mL
2 tsp	ground coriander	10 mL
2 tsp	ground cumin	10 mL
2 tbsp	soy sauce	25 mL
1 tbsp	fish sauce	15 mL
2 tbsp	lime juice	25 mL
1 tbsp	white sugar	15 mL
4	boneless, skinless chicken breasts (approx. 1 lb/500 g)	4

1. Mix the curry powder, turmeric, coriander, cumin, soy sauce, fish sauce, lime juice, and sugar in a small bowl. Whisk until well combined.

2. Put the chicken into a medium-sized resealable plastic bag. Pour in the marinade. Seal. Swoosh it all around.

3. Marinate in the fridge for 4 to 5 hours.

4. Go and do something fun.

5. When the time is up, preheat the oven to 375°F (190°C).

6. Pour the marinade and the chicken into a 9-inch (2.5 L) square baking dish.

7. Bake for 20 to 25 minutes, basting every 10 minutes. The chicken is cooked when the meat is no longer pink inside. Serve with cooked marinade over top.

Serving Suggestions
- Curried Rice with Fresh Cilantro (page 70)
- Carrots (page 55)

hicken Curry with Vegetables

Serves 4–6 (may be doubled)

I am constantly disappointed in the spiciness level of foods. When I try a new recipe that says it's "going to blow your head off," I want it to be very, very hot—but that's not always the case.

I think we should have a spicy meter as follows:

1	mild
2	
3	starting to warm up
4	
5	
6	hot mild sweats
7	
8	very hot sweats
9	
10	blow your head off

If we made it a national standard, you could pick up any recipe or eat at any restaurant knowing just how hot and sweaty you were going to get.

According to this guideline, this recipe is a 6.5.

* *If you're concerned about the fat, substitute with low-fat canned coconut milk.*

Marinade

1 tsp	paprika	5 mL
1 tsp	ground coriander	5 mL
½ tsp	ground cumin	2 mL
1 tsp	red pepper flakes	5 mL
1 tsp	turmeric	5 mL
½ tsp	white pepper	2 mL
	Juice of 2 limes	
4	boneless, skinless chicken breasts (approx. 1 lb / 500 g), chopped into 2-inch (5 cm) cubes	4

Sauce

1 tbsp	canola oil	15 mL
1 tbsp	butter	15 mL
2	large onions, coarsely chopped	2
2	cloves garlic, minced	2
1	can (14 oz / 398 mL) coconut milk*	1
3 tbsp	fish sauce	45 mL
1 tbsp	garam masala	15 mL
4	medium potatoes, peeled and quartered	4
½ lb	green beans	250 g
½ lb	baby carrots	250 g
½ cup	frozen peas	125 mL

Rice

1 cup	basmati rice	250 mL
2 cups	water	500 mL

1. In a non-metallic bowl, mix all the marinade ingredients together.

2. Add the chicken pieces. Toss to coat. Marinate, covered, in the fridge for 4 hours.

3. When the chicken is ready, heat the oil and butter in a large pot. Add the onions and sauté for 3 minutes or until translucent.

4. Add the garlic and continue sautéing—take care not to let the garlic burn.

5. Add the coconut milk, fish sauce, garam masala, and the marinated chicken. Stir. Bring to a boil. Cover and reduce heat; simmer for 20 minutes.

6. Remove chicken and keep warm. Add the potatoes, green beans, and carrots. Return to a boil. Cover and reduce heat; simmer until the potatoes are cooked, approximately 20 minutes. Return the chicken to the pot. Add the peas, cover and continue simmering for 5 minutes.

7. Following package instructions, cook the rice with the water in a separate pot. (I know you know that, but just in case.)

8. When the rice is tender, remove from heat. Let sit for 5 minutes.

9. Fluff the rice with a fork.

10. I like to serve this curry dish in bowls, but it goes onto a plate just fine! Divide the rice equally between the bowls or plates. Ladle on the chicken curry.

Serving Suggestions
- *Mixed Baby Greeens with Mango Chutney Dressing (page 25)*
- *Dessert—Fresh fruit*

Turkey with Capers and Brown Mushrooms

Serves 4–6 (may be doubled)

I used to think capers were small fish! Imagine my surprise when I discovered they were a pickled flower bud. (Just goes to show you—nobody's perfect.)

1	boneless, skinless turkey breast (approx. 2 lb/ 1 kg)	1
¼ cup	all-purpose flour	50 mL
	Salt and pepper	
2 tbsp	olive oil	25 mL
1 tbsp	butter (optional)	15 mL
½ lb	cremini mushrooms, thinly sliced	250 g
2	cloves garlic, minced	2
¼ cup	finely chopped fresh parsley	50 mL
1 tbsp	balsamic vinegar	15 mL
2 tbsp	capers, rinsed	25 mL

 Serving Suggestions
- *Mashed Potatoes (page 59)*
- *Brussels Sprouts (page 49)*
- *Yams (page 61)*

1. Slice the turkey breast into 2-inch (5 cm) thick steaks. Now for the fun: you get to pound the living daylights out of the turkey. Put the turkey between two sheets of plastic wrap. Using a meat pounder or a wooden rolling pin, pound the turkey into ½-inch (1 cm) slices. It's a great way to get rid of some frustration. Having a bad day? Invite friends over so you can double the recipe! Lots more pounding.

2. Once you've flattened all the turkey steaks, dredge them in the flour and sprinkle with the salt and pepper.

3. Heat a large frying pan. Add the oil and cook the turkey on both sides.

4. When the turkey is no longer pink inside, set aside and keep warm.

5. If the pan looks dry, add the butter. Add the mushrooms to the pan. Let them brown. Stir only occasionally.

6. When browned, add the garlic. Sauté for 1 to 2 minutes.

7. Add the parsley, vinegar, and capers. Heat through. Pour over turkey and serve.

Seafood

When you're born and raised in Vancouver, it's hard not to like fish. My all-time favourite meal is poached salmon, wild and brown rice, and steamed fiddleheads. That's about as West Coast as anyone can get.

Seafood Rules—Buying Fish

1. Fish shouldn't smell fishy! It should smell clean and fresh like the ocean.
2. Scales should be on tight. If they are really falling off, don't buy that fish. It has been dead too long.
3. The eyes should be bulging out and clear. Sunken eyes—don't buy.
4. The fish should always be packed on, and in, ice.
5. When you press the flesh, it should bounce back. Lose a finger—walk away.

Seafood Rules—Cooking

1. General rule is "high temperature, short time."
2. When poaching, do it gently.
3. Overcooked fish is the absolute worst—cook until just flaky.

Seafood

Poached Salmon

Serves 4 (generous portions)

When I was growing up, every Friday a fishmonger drove around the neighbourhood in a really old, beat-up refrigerated truck, selling his wares.

My mom would go outside and order four salmon steaks and one pound of shrimp. The fishmonger—I'm sure he had a real name but we always called him "the Fishman"—would carefully pull a sockeye from the crushed ice, weigh it, and cut off four equal steaks.

To my six-year-old eyes, the Fishman was very old and weird; he scared the hell out of me. But boy, was that salmon ever good. Thirty-four years later, I still love a great piece of salmon, and fishmongers still give me the willies.

Serving Suggestions
- *Wild and Brown Rice (page 72)*
- *Pea Salad (page 29)*

2 cups	orange juice	500 mL
1	salmon fillet	1
	(approx. 1 lb/500 g)	

1. In a large, covered frying pan, bring the orange juice to a boil.

2. Divide the salmon fillet into four equal portions.

3. When the juice begins to boil, add the salmon. The juice should just cover the fillets. Cover with a lid.

4. Gently poach for 5 minutes.

5. Gently turn the fillets over. Cover. (Don't be rough or aggressive. They will fall apart. Another life lesson.)

6. Continue poaching until they are just cooked. They are done when the salmon gently flakes. This takes anywhere from 10 to 15 minutes more. The trick is to hover and keep checking. You've just spent a lot of money—the last thing you want to do is wreck them. So hover.

7. Using a slotted spoon, remove the fillets and serve.

**oached Sole with Citrus and Fresh Ginger**

Serves 2 (may be doubled)

This delicate fish is so flavourful you'll forget that it's a low-fat meal.

1	orange	1
	Prepared orange juice to make	
	1 cup (250 mL)	
1	lemon	1
	Prepared lemon juice to make	
	¼ cup (50 mL)	
1 tbsp	grated fresh ginger	15 mL
4	sole fillets	4
	(approx. 1 lb/500g)	
1 tbsp	finely chopped fresh chives	15 mL
	(optional)	

1. Zest the orange, cut it in half, and squeeze out the juice and pulp into a glass measuring cup. Discard membrane. Then add enough prepared juice to make 1 cup (250 mL) of orange juice. Repeat with the lemon, adding prepared juice to make ¼ cup (50 mL) of lemon juice.

2. In a frying pan, mix together the zest, juice, and pulp from the orange and lemon.

3. Add the ginger and bring to a boil.

4. Add the sole. Cover and reduce heat to simmer; poach for 5 to 8 minutes or until fish flakes.

5. Remove fish with a slotted spoon and keep warm.

6. Reduce the poaching liquid: crank up the heat and boil for about 5 minutes or until the liquid is reduced by at least half.

7. Pour the sauce over the fillets. Top with chives, if using.

 Serving Suggestions
- Dad's Rice Pilaf (page 67)
- Rapini (page 52)

amily-Style Sole

Serves 4–6 (may be doubled)

This dish is quick to make and totally kid-approved.

8	sole fillets (approx. 2 lb/ 1 kg)	8
1	large egg	1
¼ cup	skim milk	50 mL
2	slices whole wheat bread	2
¼ tsp	garlic powder	1 mL
¼ tsp	onion powder	1 mL
	Salt and pepper	
2–4 tbsp	canola oil	25–60 mL

Serving Suggestions for a Totally Kid-Approved Meal

- *Rice with Green Onions and Peas (page 71)*
- *Carrots (page 55)*

1. Rinse the sole and pat dry.

2. Beat the egg and milk together in a bowl large enough in which to dip the fillets.

3. Tear up the bread and throw it into a food processor. Pulse until bread crumbs are fine.

4. Mix the bread crumbs with the garlic powder, onion powder, and salt and pepper. Put the mixture in a shallow pan. I use a pie plate.

5. Heat a non-stick pan. Add enough of the oil to cook the first batch. I've given a range of amounts for the oil. I fry all of the fish in 2 tablespoons (25 mL) tops. Fish is low in fat, and frying it in lots of fat defeats the purpose of eating it. So I've given you some leeway. If you use more than 4 tablespoons (60 mL) of oil, I don't want to know.

6. When the oil is hot, dip the fillets first in the egg mixture and then in the bread crumb mixture before adding to the pan. Fry quickly—the sole is so thin it will cook in only 2 minutes a side. Flip when golden brown. When fish is flaky, serve immediately.

 *Lick the Spoon!*

Sole with Cheese and Crackers

Serves 4–6 (may be doubled)

A quick family favourite.

8	sole fillets (approx. 2 lb/ 1 kg)	8
1	large egg	1
¼ cup	skim milk	50 mL
1 tsp	Worcestershire sauce	5 mL
1 cup	cracker crumbs (I use multigrain saltines)	250 mL
½ cup	freshly grated Parmesan cheese	125 mL
1 tsp	paprika	5 mL
	Salt and pepper	
2–4 tbsp	canola oil	25–60 mL

Serving Suggestions

- *Couscous Pilaf (page 74)*
- *Broccoli, Red Pepper, and Fresh Ginger (page 50)*

1. Rinse the sole. Pat dry.

2. Beat the egg, milk, and Worcestershire together in a glass bowl big enough to dip the fillets into.

3. In a separate bowl, mix the cracker crumbs, Parmesan, paprika, salt and pepper. Place in a shallow pan.

4. Heat a non-stick pan. As I've said before, one of the reasons we eat fish is because it's low in fat. Frying it in a lot of fat is therefore a really goofy thing to do! So I've given you a range in the amount of oil: 2 to 4 tablespoons. I fry all eight pieces in 2 tablespoons (25 mL) of oil. However, if you want to use 4 tablespoons (60 mL), I won't hold it against you.

5. When the oil is hot, not smoking, dip the fillets first in the egg mixture and then in the cracker crumb mixture before adding to the pan. Fry quickly—this will take about 2 minutes a side. Flip when golden brown. When fish is flaky, serve immediately.

od with Plum Tomatoes and Peppers

Serves 4–6 (may be doubled)

I was raised on cod. It's a popular salt-water fish that frequents the Vancouver fish markets. It's reasonably priced and it lends itself to this recipe.

6	cod fillets (approx. 1½ lb/750 g)	6
1 tbsp	olive oil	15 mL
1	large onion, coarsely chopped	1
3	cloves garlic, minced	3
8	plum tomatoes, skinned* and quartered	8
1	large sweet red pepper, coarsely chopped	1
8	kalamata olives, pitted and halved	8
¼ tsp	dried basil	1 mL
¼ tsp	dried oregano	1 mL

Serving Suggestions
- Mair's House Salad (page 28)
- Rice with Green Onions and Peas (page 71)
- Swiss Chard (page 54)

1. Preheat oven to 425°F (220°C).

2. Rinse the cod. Pat dry.

3. Lightly grease a baking dish big enough for the fillets to lie in one layer; arrange fillets and set aside.

4. In a non-stick pan, heat the oil; toss in the onion and sauté for 2 minutes or until translucent.

5. Add the garlic, plum tomatoes (I skin them—you don't have to if you don't mind the skins), red pepper, olives, basil, and oregano.

6. Cook for 2 minutes; remove from heat and pour over the fillets in the baking dish.

7. Bake the fillets for 10 to 15 minutes or until the cod flakes easily. Be careful not to overcook.

> ✳ How to skin a tomato (or is it peel)? I call it **skinning** because I pour boiling water over top of them. The skins come off easily. **Peeling** to me means you use a peeler. So my book, my rules: it's called **skinning**.

Baked Cod with Garlic and Ginger

Serves 4 (may be doubled)

This dish is low fat and easy to make.

4	cod fillets	4
	(approx. 1 lb/ 500 g)	
½ tsp	red pepper flakes	2 mL
¼ cup	soy sauce	50 mL
2 tbsp	dry sherry	25 mL
1 tbsp	grated fresh ginger	15 mL
2	cloves garlic, minced	2
¼ cup	chopped fresh chives	50 mL
	(optional)	

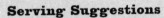

Serving Suggestions
- Mair's House Pilaf (page 69)
- Yellow and Red Peppers with Vidalia Onions (page 62)

1. Preheat oven to 425°F (220°C).

2. In an 11 x 7-inch (2 L) baking dish, lay out the cod in a single layer.

3. Sprinkle with the red pepper flakes.

4. Pour the soy sauce and the sherry over the fillets.

5. Make a paste of the ginger and garlic and spread as evenly as possible on the fillets.

6. Sprinkle the chives on top, if using.

7. Bake for 15 minutes or until the fish flakes easily. Serve.

lackened Orange Roughy with Citrus Salsa

Serves 4 (may be doubled)

Paul Prudhomme, a renowned chef out of New Orleans, has made cooking "blackened style" famous. By rubbing Cajun seasonings on fish and then cooking it in an extremely hot cast-iron pan, you end up with a crispy, spicy fish dish.

This is my recipe for blackened fish, which I serve with a cooling citrus salsa.

2½ tsp	paprika	12 mL
¼ tsp	cayenne	1 mL
¼ tsp	salt	1 mL
¼ tsp	white pepper	1 mL
4	orange roughy fillets (approx. 1½ lb/ 750 g)	4
2 tbsp	olive oil	25 mL

Citrus Salsa

1	ruby red grapefruit	1
1	navel orange	1
2 tbsp	diced red onion	25 mL
	Juice of 1 lime (1–2 tbsp/ 15–25 mL)	
1 tbsp	chopped fresh mint (optional)	15 mL
¼ tsp	white sugar	1 mL

1. Mix together the paprika, cayenne, salt, and white pepper. (This is the Cajun spice.)

2. Rinse and pat dry the orange roughy. Lay the fish on a plate and rub or pat on half the Cajun spice. Let the fish sit in the fridge while you make the citrus salsa.

3. Cut off the peel from the grapefruit and the orange. Pith and segment into a bowl. (See Methods and Techniques, page 7.)

4. Add the red onion, lime juice, mint, if using, and sugar. Gently mix together so the segments don't fall apart. Let stand while you cook the fish.

5. Heat a cast-iron frying pan until very hot. (If you don't have a cast-iron frying pan, any heavy frying pan will do.)

6. When the pan is hot, add the oil. Lay the Cajun-spiced side of the fish onto the oil. Sprinkle the remaining half of the spice mixture on top.

7. Open the windows and turn on the fan.

8. Cook the fish for approximately 4 minutes per side or until fish flakes. Serve with Citrus Salsa on top.

Serving Suggestions
- Romaine with *Avocado Dressing* (page 24)
- *Oven-Roasted Fries* (page 60)
- *Carrots* (page 55)
- Steamed broccoli

range Roughy Wrapped in Phyllo with Mango Salsa

Serves 4–6

I keep having this dream about Mel Gibson. He's at my house and he's wearing a pair of worn jeans and a white T-shirt. I am in an elegant green velvet gown that displays a lot of cleavage. (It's the best I've looked since 1981.) We are eating orange roughy in phyllo pastry. We hardly speak; our eyes are glued to each other. He finally says, "You know, Mairlyn, you have great—," and then I wake up. No kidding! I wake up in exactly the same place every darn time.

Just once I'd like to know what I have that's great.

4	orange roughy fillets (approx. 1½ lb/750 g)	4
1 tbsp	butter	15 mL
1 tsp	curry powder	5 mL
1 tsp	paprika	5 mL
1 tsp	ground cumin	5 mL
1 tsp	ground coriander	5 mL
8	sheets phyllo pastry	8
¼ cup	butter, melted	50 mL

Mango Salsa

1	large, very ripe mango	1
1	green onion, chopped	1
2 tbsp	orange juice	25 mL

1. Preheat oven to 375°F (190°C). Line a cookie sheet with parchment paper.

2. Rinse and pat dry the fillets; set aside.

3. Cream together the 1 tablespoon of butter, curry powder, paprika, cumin, and coriander; set aside.

4. Lay out one sheet of phyllo, keeping the rest under a dampened towel.

5. With a pastry brush, brush a little of the melted butter on the sheet. Lay a second sheet on top.

6. Place a fillet of the orange roughy in the bottom third.

7. Spread one-quarter of the seasoned butter on top of the fish.

8. Fold sides in and continue to fold up.

9. Lay the fish wrapped in phyllo on the cookie sheet.

10. Repeat steps 5 to 10 with the other three pieces.

11. Brush any remaining melted butter on top of each wrapped fillet.

12. Bake for 20 to 25 minutes.

13. Meanwhile, make the Mango Salsa. Peel the mango and cut the fruit from its humongous pit. Chop the pulp and add the green onion and orange juice. When phyllo packages are done, serve with the Mango Salsa on the side.

Serving Suggestions
- Rice Pilaf with Toasted Hazelnuts (page 68)
- Cucumber Salad (page 31)

urried Shrimp

Serves 4 (may be doubled)

I was raised on "Hockey Night in Canada." Every Saturday night, you could find my family watching the game while eating hamburgers my father made. It was a tradition I loved.

If I remember correctly, hockey didn't go on for most of the year back then. It was over by mid-March or so. Nowadays, the Stanley Cup—hockey's Holy Grail—is awarded sometime in June. June! For the love of Pete. Even I get tired of it.

How do I get my honey's attention when night after night he's glued to the TV? Well, I've found that serving Curried Shrimp grabs his attention for at least 15 minutes. I serve it right after Coach's Corner. The only way he'll give up Don Cherry is if I serve this dish buck naked.

It's a 5.0 on the spicy meter (see Chicken Curry with Vegetables, page 100).

> * *To clean and devein shrimp, pull off the shell with your fingers, leaving the tail intact. With a sharp paring knife, run a small cut down the back of each shrimp along the slightly visible black vein. Remove the vein— you've just deveined the shrimp. Rinse under cold water. Drain. Or, buy cleaned, deveined, tail-on shrimp.*

1 tbsp	olive oil	15 mL
4	shallots, minced	4
2 tbsp	finely grated fresh ginger	25 mL
4	cloves garlic, minced	4
1 tsp	red pepper flakes	5 mL
1 tsp	turmeric	5 mL
2 tsp	curry powder	10 mL
1½ cups	canned coconut milk	375 mL
24	cleaned, deveined raw shrimp, tails on*	24
1 cup	chopped fresh cilantro	250 mL

1. In a large frying pan, heat the oil. Toss in the shallots, ginger, and garlic; sauté until shallots are translucent. (Stir constantly so the garlic and ginger don't burn.)

2. Add the red pepper flakes, turmeric, and curry powder. Stir well. (This is a very aromatic dish.)

3. Slowly add the coconut milk. Stir well. Bring to a boil and cook for 1 minute.

4. Add the shrimp and cook at a gentle boil until shrimp are done on one side. Takes 1 to 2 minutes. Flip the shrimp over and cook on the other side until done.

5. Add the cilantro and stir until mixed in. Serve on a bed of rice.

 Serving Suggestions

- *Greens and Grapefruit (page 26)*
- *Rice with Green Onions and Peas (page 71)*
- *During hockey season—buck naked*

Vegetarian Entrées

By this point, you might be wondering, "Where's the beef?" All I can say is, it's not in my book.

> Me: Hi! My name is Mairlyn and I was a lacto-ovo-vegetarian for 15 years.
> Audience (in unison): Hi, Mairlyn.

Sound like a 12-step program? Well, most people still think vegetarians are weird, hippie types who don't pay their taxes and who wear all-cotton clothing.

I was a milk- and egg-eating vegetarian for 15 years, and I'd like to address these issues: I think weird is a relative term. I was too young to be a hippie (see Carrot Cake, page 180). I pay my taxes and . . . well . . . okay . . . I do try to wear all-cotton clothing.

For many people, vegetarianism is a conscious decision towards better health and a better environment. You don't have to grow your own sprouts and give up shaving any type of body hair to be a vegetarian. Membership is open; all you need to do is start eating less meat. Try giving meat up for one day.

What? No meat? Eat vegetarian? Before you run away screaming, consider what one day's worth of meals might be like if you were a lacto-ovo-vegetarian.

Breakfast
- Wholegrain cereal with milk
- Orange juice—you need the vitamin C for your body to absorb the iron in the cereal
- Sliced banana or fruit
- Herbal tea

Lunch
- Split pea or lentil soup

or

- Cheese, lettuce, and tomato sandwich—with sprouts? Or without.

or

- Scrambled egg
- Milk or juice

Snack
- Yogurt

or

- 6 almonds—source of calcium

or

- Dried fruit

Dinner
- Vegetarian Chili
- Quick Dinner Bread
- Steamed broccoli or green salad
- Milk or juice
- Fruit and Better-Than-Sex Brownies

Sounds pretty good. I was a vegetarian until I was pregnant with my son. During my pregnancy, I had cravings for salmon and shrimp, and once I ate deep-fried chicken with hot sauce all over it.

Today I cook vegetarian three times a week. I give my son the choice between what I'm eating or fish or chicken. Half the time he picks what I'm eating. Being a vegetarian is a healthy choice as long as you do some research on it. I recommend *Becoming Vegetarian*, the Moosewood cookbooks, *The Enchanted Broccoli Forest*, and *Cooking Vegetarian*. They are all great books filled with information you need to know. Hope you give it a whirl.

Hint—Big Hint

Beano: A little anti-gas trick. This solution contains an enzyme that helps prevent the gas attack most non-bean eaters get after eating beans. You can buy it at health food stores or some drugstores. It really works.

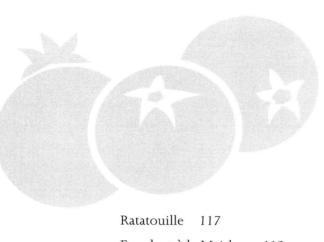

Vegetarian Entrées

Ratatouille

Serves 6

Oh, to be in Provence during eggplant season!

Ratatouille is a Mediterranean vegetable stew that I love. It combines eggplant, zucchini, sweet peppers, and plum tomatoes in garlic and olive oil. I know most people would rather be in England during cherry blossom time, but one taste of this and you'll be jumping on the Chunnel.

1	medium eggplant, cubed and sweated (see Eggplant Rules, page 120)	1
2	medium zucchini, chopped	2
1	medium red onion, chopped	1
1	large sweet red pepper, chopped into large chunks	1
3	cloves garlic, minced	3
1 tbsp	olive oil	15 mL
1	can (28 oz/796 mL) plum tomatoes, drained, OR 10 plum tomatoes, peeled	1
½ tsp	dried thyme	2 mL
½ cup	freshly grated Parmesan cheese	125 mL

1. In a big pot, sauté the eggplant, zucchini, onion, red pepper, and garlic in the olive oil.

2. Add the well-drained tomatoes and thyme. Stir. Reduce the heat to simmer and cook, covered, for 20 minutes or until the vegetables are tender.

3. Heat up broiler.

4. Spoon the ratatouille into a 9 x 13-inch (3.5 L) baking dish. Sprinkle with the Parmesan cheese. Broil until cheese bubbles. Watch it carefully—the cheese starts to bubble quickly.

5. Let sit for 5 minutes. Serve.

Pitfall *The ratatouille looks like soup. You didn't drain the tomatoes. This is fixable. Spoon out the ratatouille with a slotted spoon. Reserve the liquid for soup.*

Serving Suggestions
- *Lots of thick, crusty French bread*
- *A good bottle of red wine*

# Eggplant à la Mairlyn

Serves 6–8

One of my goals as a TV cook is to introduce you to foods you may not have tried. Eggplant is on the "Top Ten List" of vegetables that people are curious about, buy, and then let rot in the back of their fridge.

So here I am, the food fairy, to tap you on the shoulder and yell quietly in your ear, "It's just an eggplant. It's not an anaconda!"

David Letterman has a Top Ten List—well, so do I. Here are the Top Ten Reasons People Don't Buy Eggplants.

10. They had a bad eggplant experience back in the seventies they've never recovered from.

9. It's purple.

8. They heard a rumour that eggplants are really high in cholesterol.

7. Fear of salting.

6. They don't know how to pick one out.

5. They are bitter—both the eggplant and the person.

4. It's purple.

3. They were once hit in the head by a flying eggplant at a rock concert.

2. Morbid fear of new vegetables.

1. It's purple.

Okay, big deal—it is purple. Get over it. Follow these steps to a successful eggplant experience.

Eggplant Rules

1. Buy small, firm, shiny eggplants.

2. Eat no later than 1 to 2 days after you went to all that trouble of picking out a small, firm, shiny one.

3. "Sweat" the eggplant. Cut into ½-inch (1 cm) slices. Layer in a colander in the sink: eggplant, salt, eggplant, salt. How much salt? Just get the shaker out and shake as if you were going to eat it right then and there. This salting or sweating helps to take away any bitter flavour. Let it sit in the colander for 20 minutes. Rinse well. Very well. Rinse again. It's now ready for any eggplant recipe you have. So, let's start with mine.

3	medium eggplants	3
	(approx. 3 lb/ 1.5 kg)	
3 tbsp	olive oil	45 mL
1	can (28 oz/796 mL)	1
	plum tomatoes	
4	cloves garlic, minced	4
Pinch	dried thyme	Pinch
2 cups	grated Gruyère	500 mL
	or strong white Cheddar	

1. Slice and sweat the eggplant (see Eggplant Rules, above).

2. You are using only 3 tablespoons (45 mL) of oil to fry or grill the eggplant. Use a non-stick pan—that will help—and really divvy the oil out. Or barbecue with no oil at all. This frying or grilling takes 20 to 30 minutes. There's a lot of eggplant to cook.

3. Meanwhile (depending on how talented you are at doing two things at the same time), in a medium-sized pot, crush the tomatoes. Add the garlic and thyme. Simmer, uncovered, for 20 minutes.

4. Preheat the oven to 425°F (220°C).

5. When all the eggplant has been cooked, begin the layering process. In an 11 x 7-inch (2 L) baking dish, spoon half of the tomato sauce into the bottom of the pan. Layer half the eggplant—overlapping is okay. Sprinkle with half the cheese. Repeat: tomato sauce, eggplant, and cheese. Leave uncovered.

6. Bake for 25 to 35 minutes or until golden brown and bubbling. Let rest for 10 to 15 minutes. Slice and serve.

 Pitfall *It's too salty. Well, you didn't rinse it well, as I mentioned in Eggplant Rules, so I'm not taking any blame for this one. Serve with lots of red wine. Maybe everyone will be too bombed to notice.*

Serving Suggestions
- *New Wave Spinach Salad—serve as a first course (page 23)*
- *Quick Dinner Bread (page 138)*

Vegetarian Chili

**Serves 4–6
(with enough to freeze)**

President Lyndon B. Johnson loved "his bowl of red"—chili. His was the "authentic chili," which is simply chopped sirloin cooked in tomatoes and spices, with not a bean to be seen.

½ cup	Textured Vegetable Protein (TVP)*	125 mL
	Boiling water	
1 tbsp	olive oil	15 mL
1	large onion, coarsely chopped	1
3	cloves garlic, minced	3
1	large sweet red pepper, chopped	1
½ lb	small button mushrooms	250 g
1	can (28 oz/796 mL) plum tomatoes, not drained	1
1	can (19 oz/540 mL) red kidney beans, drained and rinsed	1
1	can (19 oz/540 mL) black beans, drained and rinsed	1
2 tsp	chili powder (or to taste)	10 mL
½ tsp	ground cumin	2 mL
½ tsp	ground coriander	2 mL
1 cup	tomato paste (optional)	250 mL

TVP looks like brown, coarsely crumbled crackers when it's dry and like cooked ground beef when it's reconstituted with boiling water. I use TVP in spaghetti sauces, lasagna, and chili. You can usually find it at a bulk store.

1. To a glass measuring cup containing ½ cup (125 mL) of TVP, add enough boiling water to make 1 cup. Let stand for 10 minutes or until you've added everything else to the pot.

2. In a Dutch oven or large pot, sauté in the oil the onion and garlic for 2 minutes or until the onion is translucent.

3. Add the red pepper and whole mushrooms and sauté for 2 minutes. I leave the mushrooms whole so the picky eaters in my household who don't like mushrooms can pick them out. I got tired of hearing "Yuck—I just ate a mushroom. I'm going to be sick."

4. Add the plum tomatoes, chopping them in the pot.

5. Add the kidney and black beans.

6. Add the chili powder. If kids are eating this, 2 teaspoons (10 mL) is perfect. Adults who like spice? Add more chili powder, to taste, and stir.

7. Add the cumin and coriander; stir.

8. Is the 10 minutes up? If so, add the TVP. Stir and bring to a boil.

9. Cover and turn the heat down; simmer for 1 hour.

10. If you think the chili is too liquidy, add the tomato paste, stir, and heat through. I like it the way it is.

Serving Suggestions
- *Quick Dinner Bread (page 138)*
- *Steamed broccoli*
- *Beano*

plit Pea Soup, Semi-vegetarian Style

Serves 4–8

I also call this dish Snowy Sunday Soup because we eat this in winter. The recipe makes a huge pot so, if we don't finish it off that night, I freeze the rest for lunch. This is very thick soup—a stick-to-your-ribs kind of meal.

6 cups	chicken stock	1.5 L
2 cups	yellow split peas	500 mL
8	large carrots, chopped	8
3	large onions, chopped	3
1 tsp	sea salt	5 mL

1. In a very large pot or soup kettle, mix the stock (the semi-vegetarian part—true vegetarians can use vegetable stock), split peas, carrots, onions and salt. Bring to a boil.

2. Skim off any foam. (It's a gas maker!)

3. When most of the foam has been removed, cover the pot. Reduce heat to simmer and cook for 3 to 4 hours, stirring occasionally.

4. Now—to purée or not to purée? If you have kids, leave the soup alone. There are so many carrots in it they won't know it's split pea soup. No kids? Purée and serve.

Serving Suggestions
- Mair's House Salad (page 28)
- Scones (page 141)

panish Beans and Rice

Serves 4 as a main course, 8 as a side dish

Beans give you gas. It's as simple as that. It really doesn't matter how much you pretend they don't, let's face it—beans even give women gas! So let's get it out in the open and admit—we do blart. Okay?

Now, get over it and make this absolutely delicious vegetarian dish. Serve it by candlelight—even vegetarians can be romantic.

1	medium onion, chopped	1
3	cloves garlic, crushed	3
1 tbsp	olive oil	15 mL
1 cup	short-grain brown rice	250 mL
1 tsp	saffron	5 mL
1	can (28 oz/796 mL) plum tomatoes (don't drain)	1
1	can (14 oz/398 mL) red kidney beans (don't drain)	1
1	large carrot, peeled and grated	1
¼ cup	couscous	50 mL
½ tsp	paprika	2 mL
Pinch	cayenne	Pinch
2 cups	cooked peas	500 mL

1. In a Dutch oven or large pot, sauté the onions and garlic in the olive oil until the onions are translucent.

2. Stir in the brown rice and saffron. Coat with the oil. Cook, stirring, for 1 minute.

3. Add the tomatoes, kidney beans, and carrot.

4. Bring to a boil. Cover. Reduce heat and simmer. Cook for 60 minutes.

5. Add the couscous. Stir. Cover and cook for 20 minutes.

6. Remove from heat. Add the paprika and cayenne. Stir once. Cover and let stand for 5 minutes.

7. Stir in the cooked peas and serve.

Pitfall Don't substitute white rice for brown. White rice absorbs less water, so you'll end up with a watery dish that tastes like mush! Brown rice is a much healthier choice and it's worth the wait.

Serving Suggestions
- Green salad and whole wheat bread
- Never serve this on a first date

Note Remember, there's always Beano.

Option #1 If you love cheese, serve this dish with a generous sprinkling of strong Cheddar cheese.
Option #2 Try a combo of grated Cheddar and Monterey Jack cheese.

Roasted Tofu and Potatoes

Serves 4

One of these days, I'm going to write a cookbook called "What the Heck *is* Tofu?" It would be filled with nice, non-threatening recipes using that white stuff many of you avoid in the produce section.

Okay, so what is tofu, anyway? Tofu is to soybeans what cottage cheese is to milk. When Little Miss Muffet sat on her tuffet, she was eating curds and whey—or cottage cheese and the leftover liquid. Little Miss *Soybean* Muffet would be eating tofu and leftover soybean liquid: tofu is the curds from cooked soybeans.

Most people I know don't like tofu because of its texture, not its taste. (Tofu has very little taste at all: it's the King of Bland. It takes its flavour from the foods it's cooked with—it's the voyeur of the bean world.) They complain that it's gushy, slimy, or too soft. Well, they are probably buying the wrong kind of tofu. Tofu comes in four textures: silken, soft, firm, and extra firm. I cook with firm and extra firm when I make an entrée, and use soft or silken in desserts, dips, and shakes.

These tofu critics must be stir-frying with soft tofu and ending up with a tofu slime-out. Then they're off it for good. That's like using chocolate syrup instead of chocolate chips in a cookie recipe. It would be a delicious albeit slimy mess. Okay, bad example, but I hope you see my point.

I use tofu a lot. Mostly, I marinate firm tofu in soy sauce, oyster sauce, and a little hot sauce, and then I stir-fry it. But, I also like to bake it. When baking, I pour soy sauce and oyster sauce over it, grate on some fresh ginger, and add some crushed garlic. After 20 minutes, it's ready.

The following recipe is for roasted tofu with a more Western flavour.

4	baking potatoes	4
	(approx. 1½ lb/750 g)	
1 lb	firm tofu	500 g
¼ cup	olive oil	50 mL
1 tbsp	Worcestershire sauce	15 mL
2 tsp	garlic powder	10 mL
½ tsp	paprika	2 mL
1 tsp	chili powder	5 mL
¼ tsp	pepper	1 mL

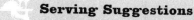

Serving Suggestions
- *Pea Salad (page 29)*
- *Scones (page 141)*

1. Preheat oven to 375°F (190°C). Line a cookie sheet with parchment paper.

2. Peel the potatoes and cut each into eight chunks.

3. Cut tofu into chunks the same size as the potatoes.

4. In a bowl, mix the potatoes and tofu.

5. Pour the oil over. Gently toss.

6. Sprinkle over the Worcestershire sauce, garlic powder, paprika, chili powder, and pepper. Toss gently to coat.

7. Spread out on pan.

8. Roast for 1½ hours until golden brown. Turn occasionally. Serve.

exican Lasagna

Serves 4

When Italy meets Mexico in soccer, it's very watchable. Well, this lasagna is very eatable: it's a great, quick meal.

3	medium zucchini, sliced lengthwise, ¼-inch thick	3
1 cup	frozen or fresh corn	250 mL
1 cup	ricotta cheese	250 mL
2½ cups	grated Monterey Jack cheese	625 mL
½ tsp	ground cumin	2 mL
3	tortilla shells, 10-inch diameter	3
1½ cups	Salsa (see page 17)	375 mL
¼ cup	chopped fresh cilantro	50 mL
1	jar (11 oz/314 mL) roasted red peppers	1

1. Preheat oven to 500°F (260°C). Lightly grease a 9 x 13-inch (3.5 L) pan. Lay the zucchini in a single layer.

2. In an 8 x 8-inch (2.0 L) pan, spread out the corn. You are going to lightly roast the zucchini and the corn to give them great flavour and to partially cook the zucchini.

3. Roast for 10 to 15 minutes. They should both have some brown colour on them. Set aside. Reduce oven temperature to 350°F (180°C).

4. While the zucchini and corn are roasting, in a medium-sized bowl, mix together the ricotta, 1½ cups (375 mL) of the Monterey Jack cheese, and the cumin.

5. Now the layering. Lightly grease an 8 x 8-inch (2.0 L) baking dish that has a lid (or you can cover it with foil).

6. Place one tortilla on the bottom. Layer ½ cup (125 mL) of the salsa, half of the cheese mixture, 1 tablespoon (15 mL) of the cilantro, one-third of the jar of roasted peppers, half of the zucchini, and half of the corn. Repeat one more layer of tortilla, ½ cup (125 mL) of the salsa, the other half of the cheese mixture, 1 tablespoon (15 mL) of the cilantro, another third of the red peppers, and the rest of the zucchini and corn.

7. Trim the last tortilla so it fits nicely on top of all those wonderful layers. Gently press down. Top with the last of the salsa, cilantro, red peppers, and the 1 cup (250 mL) of grated Monterey Jack that has been patiently sitting all alone on the counter.

8. Cover and bake for 40 minutes. When it's cooked, remove from the oven and wait for 10 to 15 minutes before you cut into it. Enjoy.

Pitfall *You cut it and it fell apart. You didn't wait long enough! It really needs to set for 10 to 15 minutes before you attack it.*

Serving Suggestions
- Romaine with *Avocado Dressing* (page 24)
- *Nacho chips*

 **rittata**

Serves 2–4

Frittatas are the quiches of the nineties. They are lighter mainly because they are not sitting on pastry. I serve them for luncheons, light dinners, or brunch.

½ lb	asparagus	250 g
1 tbsp	butter	15 mL
3	shallots, minced	3
½	large sweet red pepper, chopped	125 mL
4	large eggs	4
1 tsp	dry mustard	5 mL
1 cup	grated strong white Cheddar	50 mL

 Serving Suggestion
- *Any of my salads* **except** *Potato Salad or Cucumber Salad*

1. Preheat oven to 375°F (190°C). Lightly grease a non-metallic 8-inch (2 L) pie plate.

2. Snap off the woody ends of the asparagus. Bring a pot of water to boil. Add the asparagus and cook for 2 minutes. Remove and drain. Chop into 2-inch (5 cm) pieces.

3. In a frying pan, melt the butter. Toss in the shallots and red pepper and sauté for 2 minutes or until just tender.

4. In a medium-sized bowl, beat the eggs and mustard together.

5. Add the cooked shallots and red pepper to the eggs.

6. Add the asparagus and cheese to the bowl and stir. Pour into the pie plate.

7. Bake for 20 to 25 minutes or until set in the centre and golden brown. Serve immediately, as it deflates quickly. (Don't go there.)

Muffins
and Quick Breads

Anyone remember Grade 8 foods? Your perfect Home Ec. teacher? The Muffin Method? Well, if any of you were my former students, you'd better remember the Muffin Method. I certainly hope I drilled that into your heads.

For all those people who weren't lucky enough to have me as their Home Ec. teacher, here's the crash course.

Muffin Method
1. Wash your hands.
2. Measure all the dry ingredients into one bowl. Mix.
3. Measure all the wet ingredients into another bowl. Mix.
4. Dump all of the wet ingredients into the dry ingredients, and stir until just combined.
5. Bake.
6. Slightly cool.
7. Eat.

That's it. The Muffin Method. Five weeks of Grade 8, five minutes today. Knowing this multipurpose method will mean you should be able to make everything in this section.

Please review. There is a test.

Test
1. Explain the muffin method.

2. Name three possible wet ingredients:
   1. eggs
   2.
   3.

3. You should mix the batter
   1. a lot
   2. counterclockwise facing NE
   3. until just combined

Answers are on the bottom of the page. When you get 100 percent, you may proceed.

> **Note** Sometimes sugar becomes a wet ingredient. I found that it just blends a whole lot better when it dissolves.

Deluxe Bran Muffins

Makes 2 dozen

These muffins are deliciously moist and packed with fibre. If you aren't used to a lot of fibre, eat only one or two of these a day, if you catch my drift. Freeze the rest in a double plastic bag.

Dry Ingredients

2½ cups	whole wheat flour	625 mL
1 cup	ground walnuts	250 mL
½ cup	wheat germ	125 mL
2 tsp	baking powder	10 mL
1½ cups	bran	375 mL

Wet Ingredients

2	large eggs	2
1 cup	canola oil	250 mL
½ cup	molasses	125 mL
1 cup	low-fat yogurt	250 mL
1 cup	skim milk	250 mL
1½ cups	brown sugar	375 mL
2 tsp	baking soda	10 mL

1. Preheat oven to 375° (190°C). Line muffin tins with paper muffin cups.

2. Mix the dry ingredients together in a large bowl.

3. Mix the wet ingredients together in a separate bowl. Add the baking soda. This mixture will bubble up. Don't worry—it's supposed to.

4. Add the wet ingredients to the dry ingredients and stir until just combined.

5. Spoon into muffin tins.

6. Bake for 15 to 20 minutes or until a toothpick inserted comes out clean.

anana Bran Muffins

Makes 1 dozen

These are low-fat and high-fibre muffins. They taste best right out of the oven.

Dry Ingredients

1 cup	whole wheat flour	250 mL
1 cup	bran	250 mL
2½ tsp	baking powder	12 mL
1 tsp	cinnamon	5 mL
½ cup	currants	125 mL

Wet Ingredients

1	large egg	1
2 tbsp	canola oil	25 mL
1¼ cups	mashed bananas*	300 mL
¼ cup	molasses	50 mL
¼ cup	brown sugar	50 mL
½ cup	skim milk	50 mL

* Buy the black, yucky ones you find in the discount fruit section. They are gross and totally perfect for this recipe.

1. Preheat oven to 400°F (200°C). Line muffin tins with paper muffin cups.

2. Mix together all the dry ingredients in a medium-sized bowl.

3. Mix together all the wet ingredients in a separate bowl.

4. Add the wet ingredients to the dry ingredients and stir until just combined.

5. Spoon into muffin tin.

6. Bake for 15 to 20 minutes or until a toothpick inserted comes out clean.

range Muffins

Makes 1 dozen

This is an orangey muffin with a streusel topping.

Streusel Topping

1 tbsp	brown sugar	15 mL
1 tsp	cinnamon	5 mL
½ cup	chopped walnuts	125 mL
	Zest of one orange	

Dry Ingredients

2 cups	all-purpose flour	500 mL
1 tbsp	baking powder	15 mL
1 tsp	cinnamon	5 mL
	Zest of one orange	

Wet Ingredients

2	large eggs	2
¾ cup	skim or homogenized milk	175 mL
¼ cup	frozen orange juice concentrate, thawed	50 mL
½ cup	canola oil	125 mL
1 cup	brown sugar	250 mL

1. Preheat oven to 375°F (190°C). Line the muffin tin with paper muffin cups.

2. Mix the streusel topping ingredients together in a small bowl. Set aside.

3. Mix together all the dry ingredients in a medium-sized bowl.

4. Mix together all the wet ingredients in a separate bowl.

5. Add the wet ingredients to the dry ingredients and stir until just combined.

6. Spoon into muffin tin.

7. Sprinkle on streusel topping.

8. Bake for 20 to 23 minutes or until a toothpick inserted comes out clean.

hole Wheat Pancakes

O.K,

Makes 12 medium

I've raised my seven-year-old son on these. I first served him my pancakes when he was two. You will always know if something is good or bad when you give it to a two-year-old. Good—they gobble it up. Bad—the floor is wearing it. These pancakes have never hit the floor.

Dry Ingredients

1¼ cups	whole wheat flour	300 mL
2 tbsp	white sugar	25 mL
1 tbsp	baking powder	15 mL
1 cup	blueberries (optional)	250 mL

Wet Ingredients

1	large egg	1
1 cup	skim or soy milk	250 mL
½ cup	applesauce	125 mL

1. Mix together all the dry ingredients in a medium-sized bowl. Add blueberries, if using.

2. Mix together all the wet ingredients in a separate bowl.

3. Add the wet ingredients to the dry ingredients and stir until just combined.

4. Heat up a non-stick frying pan and lightly grease pan, if desired. Drop the batter by tablespoons onto the hot pan. Cook on one side until the surface is full of bubbles. Then turn and brown the other side.

5. Indulge in Canadian heritage and serve with real maple syrup.

ot-Whole-Wheat Pancakes

Makes approximately 12 pancakes

I decided to include a pancake recipe that is made with all-purpose flour and oil. My sister, Kathleen, thinks whole-wheat-flour recipes are weird. She eats them, mind you—but she never buys whole wheat flour. This recipe is for all the Kathleens out there.

Dry Ingredients

1 cup	all-purpose flour	250 mL
1 tbsp	baking powder	15 mL
2 tbsp	white sugar	25 mL
2 tsp	cinnamon	10 mL
1 cup	blueberries (optional)	250 mL

Wet Ingredients

1	large egg	1
2 tbsp	canola oil	25 mL
1 cup	skim or homogenized milk	250 mL

1. Mix together all the dry ingredients in a medium-sized bowl. Add blueberries, if using.

2. Mix together all the wet ingredients in a separate bowl.

3. Add the wet ingredients to the dry ingredients and stir until just combined.

4. Heat up a non-stick frying pan and lightly grease pan, if desired. Drop the batter by tablespoons into the pan. Cook on one side until the surface is full of bubbles. Then turn and brown the other side.

5. Serve with real maple syrup.

uick Dinner Bread

Makes 1 loaf

Don't have time to make a loaf of yeast bread? Well, all is not lost: make my quick bread instead. It's delicious and it goes well with chili or soup.

Dry Ingredients

2 cups	whole wheat flour	500 mL
1½ tsp	baking powder	7 mL
½ tsp	baking soda	2 mL
1 tbsp	white sugar	15 mL
1 tbsp	brown sugar	15 mL

Wet Ingredients

1	large egg	1
¾ cup	yogurt	175 mL
2 tbsp	canola oil	25 mL

1. Preheat oven to 375°F (190°C). Lightly grease a cookie sheet or line with parchment paper.

2. Mix together all the dry ingredients in a medium-sized bowl.

3. Mix together all the wet ingredients in a separate bowl.

4. Add the wet ingredients to the dry ingredients and stir until just combined.

5. Flour a board and lightly knead the bread six times.

6. Shape into a round loaf about 2 inches (5 cm) thick. Using a sharp knife, make an X in the centre of the loaf.

7. Bake for 30 to 35 minutes or until done golden brown. (The bread should sound hollow when tapped.) Serve.

anana Bread

Makes 1 loaf

I've been making this bread since my teaching days in North Vancouver. One of my claims to fame is that Brett Hull was in my Grade 9 foods class one year. I'll never forget the kids telling me he was Bobby Hull's son! They were so excited. I looked at him and said, "Yeah, right, and I'm a chicken." Well, son of a gun, turned out he was Bobby Hull's son. Cluck, cluck, cluck.

Dry Ingredients

1 cup	whole wheat flour	250 mL
¼ cup	wheat germ	50 mL
¼ cup	bran	50 mL
¼ cup	all-purpose flour	50 mL
1 tsp	baking powder	5 mL
½ tsp	baking soda	2 mL

Wet Ingredients

2	large eggs	2
½ cup	canola oil	125 mL
1 cup	mashed bananas*	250 mL
¾ cup	brown sugar	175 mL

1. Preheat oven to 350°F (180°C). Lightly grease a 9 x 5-inch (2 L) loaf pan.

2. Mix together all the dry ingredients in a medium-sized bowl.

3. Mix together all the wet ingredients in a separate bowl.

4. Add the wet ingredients to the dry ingredients and stir until just combined.

5. Pour into prepared pan.

6. Bake for 40 to 45 minutes or until a toothpick inserted comes out clean.

7. Cool for 10 minutes in the pan. Remove and continue cooling.

8. Tastes great now but will be even better tomorrow.

***** I freeze whole, really ripe bananas in their peels. They turn charcoal black and look odd, but they keep really well this way. When you need one, thaw it on a plate, cut off the end, and squeeze out the banana. Simple and easy.

Lick the Spoon!
Biscuits

The Muffin Method section is over. Okay, on to the Biscuit Method. (Home Economists have a name for everything. One of my favourites is the Chocolate-Eating Method. It involves chopsticks and a marble slab!) Anyway, here's the crash course:

Biscuit Method
1. Wash hands.
2. Mix all the dry ingredients together.
3. Cut in the solid fat (butter or shortening) with a pastry blender.
4. Mix together the wet ingredients.
5. Add the wet ingredients to the dry ingredients and stir until combined.
6. Knead.
7. Bake.
8. Eat.

Scones

Makes 8 scones

I'll admit it: I make a mean scone. Okay, it took 17 attempts before I created the perfect flaky texture and tender bite. I like to think of it as three days of rewarding work with only a five-pound weight gain.

I keep forgetting—a *taste* is all I really need.

Dry Ingredients

1 cup	whole wheat flour	250 mL
1 cup	all-purpose flour	250 mL
1 tbsp	white sugar	15 mL
1 tsp	baking powder	5 mL
1 tsp	baking soda	5 mL
1 tsp	salt	5 mL

Solid Fat

⅓ cup	chilled unsalted butter	75 mL

Wet Ingredients

½ cup	buttermilk	125 mL
1	large egg	1

1. Preheat oven to 425°F (220°C). Line a cookie sheet with parchment paper or, if you don't have parchment, lightly grease.

2. Mix together the dry ingredients in a medium-sized bowl.

3. Cut in the butter with a pastry blender. (Some people use two knives but I've never had much success. Use what you are good at. Life lesson #306.)

4. Mix together the wet ingredients.

5. Add the wet ingredients to the dry ingredients and stir with a fork until combined.

6. Gather the dough into a ball and knead ten times on a lightly floured board.

7. Pat the dough into a circle about 1½ inches (4 cm) thick.

8. Cut into eight triangles.

9. Separate the triangles and put onto the cookie sheet.

10. Bake for 12 to 15 minutes or until golden brown. Serve warm.

Serving Suggestions
- Sunny afternoon
- Tea laced with Grand Marnier
- Devon cream and raspberry jam
- Pachelbel's Canon in D on the CD player

Pitfall *You replaced all-purpose flour with whole wheat flour. This is not a total disaster. The dough will just be sticky, so knead in a little extra flour.*

 raditional Biscuits

Makes 8 biscuits

I have a tea party with my girlfriends every Christmas. We eat biscuits, shortbread cookies, mince tarts, and chocolate cake, and we drink gallons of tea. I put out all my good china, crystal, and silver, and wear a velvet dress. It's so much fun to be elegantly old-fashioned and fantasize about living in Victorian England . . . and then I remember that no-indoor-plumbing thing, and I'm thrilled I live in the 1990s in Canada.

Dry Ingredients

2 cups	all-purpose flour	500 mL
2 tsp	cream of tartar	10 mL
1 tsp	baking soda	5 mL
1 tsp	baking powder	5 mL

Solid Fat

¼ cup	shortening	50 mL
2 tbsp	chilled unsalted butter	25 mL

Wet Ingredients

1	large egg	1
½ cup	homogenized milk	125 mL

1. Preheat oven to 400°F (200°C). Line a cookie sheet with parchment paper or, if you don't have parchment, lightly grease.

2. Mix together all the dry ingredients in a medium-sized bowl.

3. Cut in the shortening and butter with a pastry blender.

4. Mix together the wet ingredients.

5. Add the wet ingredients to the dry ingredients and stir with a fork until combined.

6. Gather the dough into a ball and knead ten times on a lightly floured board.

7. Pat the dough into a circle about 1½ inches (4 cm) thick.

8. Cut into eight triangles.

9. Separate the triangles and put onto a cookie sheet.

10. Bake for 10 to 12 minutes or until golden brown. Serve warm.

Cookies, Bars, and Squares

Cookies and milk. There is something very comforting about this dynamic duo.

I have a special place in my heart and a really big place on my hips where cookies dwell. Bar cookies (or brownies) were the first thing I ever baked with my mom. And the rest is history.

Cookies—of every kind—and brownies are still my favourite things to bake and eat. You know, I've often wondered how my life would have turned out if my favourites had been liver and onions.

Here are some basic cookie rules.

Cookie Rules

1. When the recipe calls for cereal flakes, any commercial breakfast cereal that is low in sugar, such as cornflakes or bran flakes, will work.

2. When the recipe says to beat in the sugar until it's creamy, beat until the sugar crystals aren't noticeable. You want a smooth, fluffy mixture, not a coarse, grainy one.

3. I always use parchment paper to line my cookie sheet. This ensures that the cookies never stick. I take the cookies out of the oven and go do something else—answer the phone and so on—and when I get back, I don't need a crowbar to pry the cookies off the pan! I love parchment paper.

4. Don't substitute wax paper for parchment unless the recipe says to.

5. Never go beyond doubling a recipe. It won't be the same.

Cookies, Bars, and Squares

Better-Than-Sex Brownies

Makes 1 huge brownie or 20 regular-sized brownies

Necessity is not the true mother of invention. PMS is. I have created the most decadent chocolate treats while under the influence of fluctuating hormone levels. Case in point—these fudgy morsels were invented on Day 26 of my cycle.

I think brownies are the ultimate quickie. You can whip them up and indulge in about 35 minutes. Men call this a marathon of passion. Women call it foreplay.

These are without a doubt *the best brownies in history*. Follow the recipe exactly, right down to baking them for 21 minutes.

Warning: Eating half the pan tends to cause headaches. Go figure.

½ cup	unsalted butter	125 mL
2 oz	semi-sweet chocolate	50 g
2 oz	unsweetened chocolate	50 g
2 oz	bitter-sweet chocolate	50 g
1 cup	white sugar	250 mL
2	large eggs	2
½ tsp	vanilla	2 mL
¾ cup	all-purpose flour	175 mL
½ tsp	baking powder	2 mL

⭐ **Bonus** They actually taste better the next day!

1. Preheat oven to 350°F (180°C). Grease an 8 x 8-inch (2 L) square pan.

2. In a medium-sized saucepan, melt together over low heat the unsalted butter and the semi-sweet, unsweetened, and bitter-sweet chocolate. Stir constantly to prevent the chocolate from scorching.

3. When just melted, remove from heat.

4. Stir in the sugar.

5. Beat in the eggs one at a time.

6. Stir in the vanilla.

7. Gently stir in the flour and baking powder.

8. Pour into the pan.

9. Bake for 21 minutes. (The brownies should be slightly underdone, since they continue to cook after they've been removed from the pan.)

10. Cool on a wire rack in the pan. Cut into squares.

11. Store in an airtight container up to 3 days—if they last that long.

☹ **Pitfall #1** It's 10:35 p.m. and all you've got is salted butter. It's okay: the brownies will be fine, but next time buy unsalted butter.

Pitfall #2 You couldn't wait until they were cool and you've burnt your tongue. Suck on an ice cube.

amily Brownies

(kid approved)

**Serves 4 chocoholics or
a regular family of 12**

There is nothing worse than a dried-out brownie—except, perhaps, gaining ten pounds due to water retention!

Brownies are a snap to make; it's the baking that usually wrecks them. Make sure your oven temperature is 350°F (180°C) and bake them for only 20 to 23 minutes. They are supposed to be under-cooked. They finish doing their thing while they are cooling. Trust me.

2 tbsp	unsalted butter	25 mL
3 tbsp	shortening	45 mL
2 oz	unsweetened chocolate	50 g
1 cup	white sugar	250 mL
2	large eggs	2
¾ cup	all-purpose flour	175 mL
½ tsp	baking powder	2 mL
¼ cup	mini chocolate chips	50 mL

1. Preheat oven to 350°F (180°C). Grease an 8 x 8-inch (2 L) square pan.

2. In a medium-sized saucepan, melt over low heat the unsalted butter, shortening, and chocolate.

3. When just melted, remove from heat.

4. Stir in the sugar.

5. Beat in the eggs, one at a time.

6. Gently stir in the flour, baking powder, and chocolate chips.

7. Pour into pan.

8. Bake for 20 to 23 minutes. (The brownies are done when they pull away from the sides of the pan, and spring back when you touch them.)

9. Cool on a wire rack in the pan. Cut into squares.

10. Store in an airtight container for 2 to 3 days.

Lemon Bars

Makes 16–24 bars

Imagine making a lemony dessert in less than one hour. Now, imagine winning the lottery. Which thought is more exciting? Okay, bad example, but face it—your chances of winning the lottery are slim to non-existent. You can, however, be eating lemon squares in 45 minutes, and they taste just like lemon meringue pie.

Base

1¼ cups	all-purpose flour	300 mL
2 tbsp	icing sugar	25 mL
⅔ cup	chilled unsalted butter, cut into small pieces	150 mL

Filling

2	large eggs	2
1 cup	white sugar	250 mL
	Zest and juice of 2 lemons	
3 tbsp	all-purpose flour	45 mL
¼ tsp	baking powder	1 mL

1. Preheat oven to 350°F (180°C). Grease an 8 x 8-inch (2 L) square pan.

2. In a food processor or blender, pulse the all-purpose flour, icing sugar, and chilled butter until the mixture looks like sawdust or sand. It should take 2 to 3 minutes.

3. Pour into pan. Pat down firmly with your hands (if you don't, it will fall apart later). Bake for 15 minutes or until just brown.

4. Meanwhile, in the food processor or blender—you don't even need to wash it—pulse the eggs, sugar, lemon zest (about 2 tablespoons/25 mL), lemon juice (about ⅓ cup/75mL), flour, and baking powder until combined.

5. As soon as the base comes out of the oven, pour the filling on top.

6. Bake for 25 minutes.

7. Cool on a wire rack in the pan. Cut into squares.

8. Store in an airtight container for 3 to 5 days.

hocolate Chip Squares
(kid approved)

Makes 24 squares

Squares—there's a flashback waiting to happen. My mom belonged to a women's group at our church, back in the days when you called everyone "Mr." and "Mrs."

For the Spring Daffodil Tea, everyone baked her special square. I adored the marshmallow square, the cherry one, and the walnut slice. I was too young to exchange recipes with "the ladies," so if any of you have a great square or slice recipe, send it to me. You'll help me re-live my childhood.

Base

1¼ cups	all-purpose flour	300 mL
¼ cup	bran	50 mL
⅓ cup	brown sugar	75 mL
¾ cup	unsalted butter, cut into cubes	175 mL

Filling

3	large eggs	3
1 cup	brown sugar	250 mL
1½ cups	flaked, unsweetened coconut	375 mL
3 tbsp	all-purpose flour	45 mL
½ tsp	baking powder	2 mL
1 tsp	vanilla	5 mL
1¼ cups	semi-sweet chocolate chips	300 mL

1. Preheat the oven to 350°F (180°C). Grease a 9 x 13-inch (3.5 L) pan.

2. In a food processor or blender, pulse the flour, bran, and brown sugar until well combined.

3. Add the cubed butter and pulse until crumbly. (Don't overpulse or dough will form.)

4. Pour the mixture into the pan; bake for 10 minutes or until just brown.

5. In the food processor or blender—you don't even have to rinse it out (what a great recipe!)—pulse the eggs, brown sugar, coconut, and flour.

6. When the base comes out of the oven, cool on a rack in the pan.

7. Add to the egg mixture the baking powder, vanilla, and chocolate chips. Pulse until combined. (And you thought I'd forgotten some ingredients.)

8. By this time, the base should be cooled. Carefully spoon out the filling onto the base, making sure that it is even.

9. Bake for 20 minutes or until done.

10. Cool completely. No sneaky little tastes. If the squares aren't completely cooled before serving, they will fall apart.

11. When the squares are cool—completely cool—cut into bars. Store in an airtight container for 2 to 4 days.

Here's the no-food-processor, no-blender method:

1. Use a pastry blender to combine the base ingredients.

2. Use a whisk to combine the filling ingredients.

My Favourite Chocolate Chip Cookies

Makes 3 dozen cookies

When I die, I'd like to be remembered for my offbeat humour, my endless knowledge of trivia, my mothering skills, and my chocolate chip cookies.

Testing chocolate chip cookies was a win-win situation. They were all good. Which were the best? Hmmmm? Better test another recipe idea.

I finally figured out that how much a person liked the cookie was directly proportional to how many chocolate chips were in each one. Ten chocolate chips—"It's good"; fifteen—"Hey, great cookie"; twenty—"These are the best cookies I've ever had. Can I have the recipe?"

Without further ado, here's a crispy, saucer-sized chocolate-packed cookie.

½ cup	unsalted butter	125 mL
¼ cup	shortening	50 mL
1¼ cups	dark brown sugar	300 mL
½ cup	white sugar	125 mL
2	large eggs	2
1 tsp	vanilla	5 mL
1½ cups	whole wheat flour	375 mL
½ tsp	baking soda	2 mL
2 cups	jumbo semi-sweet	500 mL
	chocolate chips or chunks	

1. Preheat oven to 375°F (190°C). Line a cookie sheet with parchment paper.

2. In a medium-sized bowl, cream together the butter and shortening.

3. Beat in the brown sugar until creamy.

4. Beat in the white sugar until creamy. Don't beat in the brown and the white sugar at the same time. Each sugar needs some "time alone" to blend in with the fat.

5. Beat in the eggs one at a time.

6. Beat in the vanilla. The batter should be a beige colour by now. If not, beat another minute or so.

7. Stir in the whole wheat flour and baking soda. Use whole wheat flour—all-purpose flour makes a different cookie. (See "The Other Chocolate Chip Cookie Recipe," on page 152.)

8. Add the chocolate chips or chunks and stir until combined.

9. Drop by teaspoonfuls and bake nine at a time. (They really spread out.)

10. Bake for 10 to 11 minutes or until lightly brown. Let them cool on the parchment paper for 1 to 2 minutes before transferring them to a cooling rack.

11. Store in an airtight container for 3 to 6 days or eat immediately.

Pitfall #1 *The cookies fell apart when you took them off the cookie sheet. You didn't let them cool for 1 to 2 minutes on the parchment paper. They need to set. Eat the crumbs and do the next batch, making sure to follow this all-important step.*

Pitfall #2 *The cookies stuck to the pan. You didn't use parchment paper. It's great stuff and it helps make all cookies great. Run to the store and buy a case.*

he Other Chocolate Chip Cookie Recipe

Makes 3–4 dozen

Having said that the previous chocolate chip cookie is my favourite, I know you're probably wondering why this one is even in the book.

Well, the truth is . . . this is my mother's favourite. Okay? And she *told* me to include it. Now I haven't done anything my mom has told me since I was 18, so I thought, what the heck, I'll do it. And she's right—it's a great cookie. It's made with all-purpose flour instead of whole wheat, and it's chewy not crispy.

½ cup	unsalted butter	125 mL
½ cup	brown sugar	125 mL
½ cup	white sugar	125 mL
1	large egg	1
1 tsp	vanilla	5 mL
1¼ cups	all-purpose flour	300 mL
½ tsp	baking soda	2 mL
1½ cups	semi-sweet chocolate chips	375 mL

1. Preheat oven to 375° F (190°C). Line a cookie sheet with parchment paper.

2. In a medium-sized bowl, cream the butter.

3. Beat in the brown sugar until creamy.

4. Beat in the white sugar until creamy.

5. Beat in the egg and vanilla.

6. Stir in the flour and soda. Mix until incorporated.

7. Add the chocolate chips and stir until combined.

8. Drop by teaspoonfuls and bake 12 at a time.

9. Bake for 11 to 13 minutes or until lightly brown. Let them cool on the parchment paper for 1 minute; transfer to a cooling rack.

10. Store in an airtight container for 3 to 6 days.

eanut Butter Cookies

Makes 3 dozen

Let's play a little game of word association. Say the first thing that comes into your head when you read the following words:

1. chocolate
2. cookies
3. peanuts

My word associations are (1) rich, (2) cookies, (3) movie theatres. Which reminds me—my pet peeve is people who talk in movie theatres. Or whose cell phones ring and who talk on the phone. People, stay home. Wait until the movie comes out on video. Then stay home and call someone on your cell phone and tell them the plot. Okay . . . where was I? Peanuts . . . oh yeah, here's my recipe for peanut butter cookies.

½ cup	shortening	125 mL
½ cup	crunchy peanut butter	125 mL
1 cup	brown sugar	250 mL
1	large egg	1
1 tbsp	water	15 mL
½ tsp	vanilla	2 mL
1 cup	all-purpose flour	250 mL
1 cup	salted peanuts	250 mL
½ cup	semi-sweet	125 mL
	chocolate chips (optional)	

1. Preheat the oven to 350°F (180°C). Do not grease the cookie sheet.

2. In a medium-sized bowl, cream together the shortening and peanut butter.

3. Beat in the brown sugar until creamy.

4. Beat in the egg, water, and vanilla.

5. Stir in the flour until well combined.

6. Add the peanuts and the chocolate chips, if you are using them.

7. Form teaspoonfuls with a spoon and then lightly press the cookie dough onto the cookie sheet.

8. Bake for 12 to 14 minutes or until golden brown.

9. Cool for 1 minute on the cookie sheet; remove from the pan and let them finish cooling on a rack.

10. Store in an airtight container for 3 to 6 days.

 **atmeal Saucer Cookies**

Makes 3–4 dozen

This recipe is an old stand-by at my house. Make sure you use oat flakes, not oatmeal. Oat flakes or old-fashioned oats are bigger than oatmeal, making this cookie big and crispy. I also use these cookies to make ice cream sandwiches. Just put softened ice cream between two cookies and gently press down. Roll the ice cream part in crushed chocolate and refreeze. A great kid or adult treat.

1 cup	shortening	250 mL
1 ½ cups	brown sugar	375 mL
1 tbsp	molasses	15 mL
2	large eggs	2
1 tsp	vanilla	5 mL
2 cups	oat flakes	500 mL
1 ½ cups	whole wheat flour	375 mL
1 tsp	baking soda	5 mL
1 cup	raisins or currants (optional)	250 mL
1 cup	semi-sweet chocolate chips (optional)	250 mL

1. Preheat oven to 375°F (190°C). Line a cookie sheet with parchment paper.

2. In a medium-sized bowl, cream the shortening.

3. Beat in the brown sugar and molasses until mixture looks creamy.

4. Beat in the eggs, one at a time.

5. Beat in the vanilla.

6. Stir in the oat flakes, whole wheat flour, and baking soda until combined.

7. If you are going to use the raisins, currants, or chocolate chips (some or all of them), add them now and stir until combined.

8. Drop by teaspoonfuls 3 inches (8 cm) apart—they really spread out.

9. Bake for 10 to 14 minutes or until lightly browned.

10. Remove right away to a wire rack and cool.

11. Store in an airtight container for 3 to 6 days.

Whoopee Cookies

Makes 30–36 cookies

I first started using this recipe when I was a student teacher. I told the kids we were going to make healthy cookies, and they all said "whoopee," sounding more like dead fish than live Grade 8 students.

Well, they quickly discovered that these cookies were excellent—especially the batter. What kid doesn't know that cookie dough is great? So you get worms—who cares? Oh, to be young again.

¼ cup + 2 tbsp	unsalted butter	90 mL
¼ cup + 2 tbsp	brown sugar	90 mL
¼ cup + 2 tbsp	white sugar	90 mL
1	large egg	1
1 tsp	vanilla	5 mL
½ cup	raisins	125 mL
½ cup	flaked, unsweetened coconut	125 mL
½ cup	cereal flakes	125 mL
½ cup	old-fashioned rolled oats	125 mL
¾ cup	whole wheat flour	175 mL
¼ tsp	baking soda	1 mL
¼ tsp	baking powder	1 mL

1. Preheat oven to 375°F (190°C). Line a cookie sheet with parchment paper.

2. In a medium-sized bowl, cream the butter.

3. Beat in the brown and white sugar until it's very, very creamy, 3 to 5 minutes.

4. Beat in the egg and vanilla, and then beat for 1 more minute.

5. Stir in the raisins, coconut, cereal flakes, rolled oats, whole wheat flour, baking soda, and baking powder until combined. (What? No chocolate chips? If you want, you could add 1 cup/250 mL chocolate chips.)

6. Drop by teaspoonfuls onto the cookie sheet.

7. Bake for 10 to 12 minutes or until golden brown.

8. Cool on a wire rack and store in an air-tight container for 3 to 6 days.

ingersnaps

Makes 4 dozen

One of my many food idiosyncrasies is that I bake gingersnaps only in the fall and at Christmas. It would be just too weird to eat a gingersnap if I was wearing a bikini. Actually, the *really* weird part would be me in a bikini! But you get my drift: you don't eat a fall cookie in the summer. Food Rule #9.

¾ cup	shortening	175 mL
1 cup	dark brown sugar	250 mL
1	large egg	1
¼ cup	molasses	50 mL
2¼ cups	all-purpose flour	550 mL
2 tsp	baking soda	10 mL
2 tsp	cinnamon	10 mL
1½ tsp	ground ginger	7 mL
½ tsp	ground cloves	2 mL
½ cup	white sugar	125 mL

1. Line a cookie sheet with parchment paper.

2. In a medium-sized bowl, cream the shortening.

3. Beat in the sugar until creamy.

4. Beat in the egg and molasses until creamy.

5. Stir in the flour, baking soda, cinnamon, ginger, and cloves until well combined.

6. Cover the dough in plastic wrap or put in a plastic bag. Put in the fridge for anywhere from 1 hour to 3 days.

7. When ready to bake, preheat the oven to 375°F (190°C).

8. Roll about 1½ to 2 teaspoonfuls of dough into balls. Dip the top into the white sugar.

9. Put the sugar-covered balls on the prepared cookie sheet and gently flatten with your fingers.

10. Bake for 10 to 12 minutes or until golden brown.

11. Cool on a wire rack and store in an airtight container. These keep well for up to 2 weeks.

N o-Bake Chocolate Treats

Makes 24 treats

I looked up the word *treat* in the dictionary. It says "to entertain with food." Which means as long as you are entertaining someone a treat could be anything. So smoked mackerel is a treat? I don't think so. I'm rewriting the definition. In Mairlyn's Dictionary, "a treat is a small or large snack that has chocolate in or on it."

Here, then, is a *real* treat.

1	package (11 oz/300 g)	1
	semi-sweet chocolate chips	
1 tbsp	butter	15 mL
⅔ cup	salted peanuts	150 mL
3 cups	cornflakes	750 mL

1. Line a cookie sheet with parchment paper or wax paper.

2. In a heavy saucepan over low heat, melt the chocolate chips and the butter, stirring constantly.

3. When melted, remove from heat.

4. Dump in the peanuts and cornflakes. Stir until combined.

5. Drop by teaspoonfuls onto the cookie sheet. Chill for 1 to 2 hours.

6. Store in an airtight container for 3 to 4 days.

Prep time—5 minutes.
Eating time—15 minutes.

> **Note** *This is just the easiest thing to whip up when you're having a chocolate breakdown.*

Desserts

I admit it openly: dessert is my favourite part of the meal. When I plan a dinner party, I pick the dessert first and then decide on the entrée.

When I worked on this chapter, it didn't feel like work at all. It was fat-indulging, yummy experimentation. I gained 11 pounds. (That's an entire size in jeans.) I have a pair of pants I kept from my pregnancy days; I call them my "fat pants." I had to wear them for a couple of weeks after I finished the dessert section. All in all, even though I felt like Baby Huey, it was very satisfying work.

Desserts are very special. They are the big finale. You can burn the chicken, wreck the potatoes, and serve lifeless, grey broccoli. But if the dessert is fabulous, people will believe you are a great cook.

Dessert Rules

1. Desserts are divided into two categories: family desserts and company desserts.

2. Family desserts should be on the healthy side. You know—fruit.

3. Company desserts are fattening and are not even remotely healthy. No one is going to say, "If you don't finish your chocolate fudge cake, there won't be any carrots for you, Mister."

4. Company desserts should be eaten *only* when company comes over.

5. Never make a company dessert on a family night. All that fat, sugar, and yummy chocolate will make your family unbearable to live with when you try to pawn off sliced bananas as dessert the next night.

6. Company desserts are decadent. If you are worried about budget, go with the expensive dessert and serve hot dogs as the entrée—no one will notice.

7. Company desserts do not contain any artificial ingredients. They call for real whipped cream, butter, cream cheese, chocolate, and so on.

8. Family desserts can be very good too, as long as you serve them with ice cream.

9. When you are really crabby, eat a company dessert by yourself. This may not help your mood, but it's always worth a try.

10. Believe that *dessert* is spelt with the double s on purpose. It's not a *desert*; it's a *dessert*. So indulge.

11. Too much fat will kill you.

12. Ignore rule 11, occasionally.

13. Make a conscious decision to start an aerobics plan tomorrow.

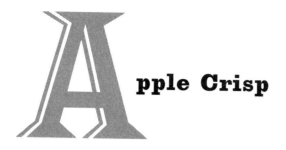

pple Crisp

Serves 4–6

In my Home Ec. class in Grade 9, we were given an assignment called the "oven dinner." Guess what it entailed? Yes, everything had to be cooked in the oven.

My Grade 9 imagination went into a cooking whirl. What to make? How do I get an A? I decided on the pioneer slant. I'd roast a chicken leg and bake potatoes and peas with the topper—pioneer apple crisp.

Everything was a big hit, except for the baked peas. Who knew they'd actually explode and then turn a ghostly grey? Those peas earned me a B+ and that was the last time I baked them, let me tell you.

I still make apple crisp whenever I roast a chicken. Every time I do, I see myself back in Grade 9 with my frizzy hair, bushy eyebrows, and hippie skirt.

Filling

6 cups	sliced peeled apples	1.5 L
¼ cup	unsweetened apple juice	50 mL
2 tbsp	brown sugar	25 mL
1 tsp	cinnamon	5 mL

Topping

1 cup	all-purpose flour or whole wheat flour	250 mL
½ cup	brown sugar	125 mL
1 tsp	cinnamon	5 mL
½ cup	butter	125 mL
½ cup	oat flakes	125 mL

1. Preheat oven to 350°F (180°C)—or move roasting chicken to one side of the already hot oven.

2. Put the sliced apples into a 9 x 9-inch (2 L) baking pan.

3. Pour the apple juice on top; sprinkle on the brown sugar and cinnamon.

4. In a medium-sized bowl, mix together the flour, brown sugar, and cinnamon. Cut in the butter with a pastry blender or with two knives. Stir in oat flakes.

5. Sprinkle the topping on top of the apples.

6. Bake for 40 to 45 minutes or until the apples are soft and the topping is golden brown. Serve warm, with or without ice cream.

Rhubarb Crisp

Serves 4–6

Crocuses, garage sales, and the first rhubarb sighting mean spring to me.

Historically, rhubarb was a spring tonic, a body cleanser. Scientifically, rhubarb is high in vitamins A and C, two vitamins pioneers would not have gotten much of during the long winters. So by the time April or May rolled around, people would be in need of a vitamin boost, which they could get by eating only the stalks—the leaves are poisonous.

Filling

5 cups	chopped rhubarb	1.25 L
½ cup	brown sugar	125 mL
½ cup	raisins	125 mL
2 tbsp	whole wheat flour	25 mL
1 tbsp	cinnamon	15 mL

Topping

1 cup	old-fashioned rolled oats	250 mL
½ cup	whole wheat flour	125 mL
½ cup	brown sugar	125 mL
1 tbsp	cinnamon	15 mL
¼ cup	canola oil	50 mL

1. Preheat oven to 350°F (180°C).

2. Put the chopped rhubarb in a 9 x 9-inch (2 L) baking pan; sprinkle with the brown sugar, raisins, flour, and cinnamon.

3. In a medium-sized bowl, mix together the rolled oats, flour, brown sugar, and cinnamon.

4. Add the oil and mix with a fork until well combined or until everything looks wet.

5. Sprinkle the topping over the rhubarb.

6. Bake for 40 to 45 minutes or until the rhubarb is soft and the topping is golden brown. Serve warm, with or without ice cream.

Sorbets

Sorbets are made from juice or puréed fruits. They are fat free (what are they doing in the dessert section?), easy as all get-out to make, and wonderfully refreshing. Sorbets are particularly great on a hot summer night, but I make them all year long.

I've included five sorbet recipes, three of which call for Simple Syrup, which you make ahead of time. You can store the syrup in the refrigerator and use it in lemonade, as a sweetener in drinks, or for more sorbet.

Simple Syrup—for Banana, Strawberry, and Raspberry Sorbets

2 cups	water	500 mL
2 cups	white sugar	500 mL

1. In a saucepan, combine the water and sugar. Heat until the sugar is completely dissolved.

2. Remove from heat. Cool. Store covered in the fridge for up to 2 weeks.

Sorbet Rules
1. Eat fast—it melts quickly.

Chocolate Banana Sorbet

Serves 4–6

When I was growing up, ice cream was my all-time favourite treat. My dad would pack us up into the car on a Sunday night, drive around Stanley Park, and end up at the Mecca of ice cream parlours—Peter's. Licking my chocolate ripple cone as slowly as I possibly could was nirvana to me.

Imagine my shock when my doctor told me I was lactose intolerant. All I could think was "Does this mean Häagen-Dazs is a bad thing?"

Since my day of milk reckoning, I have searched for an ice cream replacement, and on January 14, 1981, at 3:06 p.m., I came up with Chocolate Banana Sorbet. It's milk free and the closest thing to ice cream I've ever tasted.

4	very ripe bananas*	4
⅔ cup	Simple Syrup (page 163)	150 mL
2 tbsp	cocoa powder	25 mL

1. Purée the bananas, Simple Syrup, and cocoa powder until liquefied.

2. Pour into ice cube trays or a shallow pan.

3. Freeze for 6 hours.

4. Put frozen chunks into the food processor and purée until smooth. This step may take a while, depending on how frozen the banana mixture is. Serve immediately. If you decide to eat it right out of the food processor, remove the blade. Remember, safety first.

* Buy the black, yucky ones you find in the discount fruit section. They are gross and totally perfect for this recipe.

aspberry Sorbet

Serves 4

My neighbours and fairy godparents, Bill and Nina, used to grow raspberries. Lucky for me, the raspberry canes invaded my yard.

One of my life's simple pleasures is to go barefoot at daybreak in my nightgown to pick and eat the plump red raspberries. I've shocked many a neighbour, let me tell you.

If there are any left, I make sorbet.

1½ cups	raspberries	375 mL
⅔ cup	Simple Syrup (page 163)	150 mL
2 tbsp	lime juice	25 mL

1. Purée the raspberries, Simple Syrup, and lime juice until liquefied.

2. Pour into ice cube trays or a shallow pan.

3. Freeze for 6 hours.

4. Put the frozen chunks into the food processor and purée until smooth. Serve immediately.

# trawberry Sorbet

Serves 6–8

The hardest part about this recipe is finding a flat surface in your freezer. Oh—and never ever walk down the basement stairs to the deep freeze carrying a too-full pan of strawberry sorbet. I have never gotten the pink, sticky stuff off the brick wall.

Note *If fresh strawberries are in season, slice them and use them instead of the frozen type. You may need to add more Simple Syrup to sweeten and to help liquefy.*

2	packages (each 15 oz/425 g) frozen sliced strawberries in light syrup	2
⅔ cup	Simple Syrup (page 163)	150 mL
2 tbsp	lemon juice	25 mL

1. Purée the strawberries, Simple Syrup, and lemon juice until the strawberries are liquefied.

2. Pour into ice cube trays or a shallow pan.

3. Freeze for 6 hours.

4. Put the frozen chunks into the food processor and purée until smooth. Serve immediately. If there are any leftovers, pack into a freezer container and store in freezer. It'll keep for up to 2 weeks.

Lemon Sorbet

Serves 4

If you really want a refreshing sorbet, this would be the one. It doesn't quite "suck the spit right out of your mouth," but it's close.

1 cup	white sugar	250 mL
1 cup	water	250 mL

Zest and juice of 2 lemons

1. In a saucepan, heat the sugar and water until the sugar is dissolved.

2. Add the lemon zest and juice. (You should have about 2 tablespoons/25 mL of zest and about ⅓ cup/75 mL of juice.) Remove from heat and cool.

3. Once cool, pour into ice cube trays or a shallow pan.

4. Freeze for 6 hours.

5. Put the frozen chunks into the food processor and purée until smooth. Serve immediately.

range and Scented Geranium Sorbet

Serves 4

In 1992, I went through what I like to call "my romantic Victorian stage." I redecorated my house in an explosion of chintz and white lace. I also got hooked on Victorian scented geraniums. Their leaves give off lemon, orange, rose, and peach scents. I knew they were edible but I couldn't find a single recipe that called for their aromatic leaves.

One day, while making an orange sorbet, I hit on the idea of steeping my geranium leaves in the juice. It worked. If you don't happen to have any scented geraniums kicking around, use boring old mint.

 Most specialty herb stores or gardening centres sell scented geraniums.

⅔ cup	white sugar	150 mL
1 cup	water	250 mL
2 cups	orange juice	500 mL
¼ cup	lemon juice	50 mL
8	leaves of Victorian lemon-rose scented geraniums,* washed	8

1. In a saucepan, heat the sugar and water until the sugar is dissolved.

2. Add the orange and lemon juice. Bring to a boil.

3. Add the geranium leaves. Remove from the heat, cover, and steep for 5 minutes.

4. Remove and discard leaves. Cool.

5. Pour into ice cube trays or a shallow pan.

6. Freeze for 6 hours.

7. Put the frozen chunks into the food processor and purée until smooth. Serve immediately.

laming Vodka Orange Crêpes

Serves 4 adults

I made these at the Fifth Annual Good Food Show in Toronto. An audience member came up to be my assistant. She was a terrific sport.

All went well until the flaming part. No flame. Not even a glimmer of blue flames. So I added much more vodka. What an inferno! It was spectacular—I thought it would never go out. Luckily it did and they were the best crêpes I'd ever had.

The moral of the story? If my assistant and I can flame crêpes in front of 200 people, you can too, in the privacy and comfort of your kitchen.

Don't let all the ingredients and the number of steps throw you. This irresistible dessert is really easy to make.

Note This is an adult dessert because the oranges are soaked in vodka. So don't serve this to anyone underage, anyone on antibiotics, or anyone operating a backhoe.

Crêpe Batter

3	large eggs	3
1 ½ tbsp	white sugar	22 mL
1 tbsp	canola oil	15 mL
1 cup	water	250 mL
½ cup	table cream	125 mL
¾ cup	all-purpose flour	175 mL
1 ½ tsp	baking powder	7 mL
1 tsp	cinnamon	5 mL
	Freshly grated nutmeg (optional)	

Flambé Sauce

2	oranges	2
2 tbsp + ¼ cup	vodka	25 mL + 50 mL
¼ cup	unsalted butter	50 mL
½ cup	marmalade	125 mL
3 tbsp	white sugar	45 mL
1 tbsp	lemon juice	15 mL
⅓ cup	orange juice	75 mL

Crêpes

1. In a medium-sized bowl, beat together the eggs, sugar, oil, water, and table cream.

2. Beat in the flour, baking powder, cinnamon, and nutmeg, if using. Beat for at least 2 minutes. Let sit for 5 minutes or as long as 1 hour in the refrigerator. The bubbles will disappear and the crêpes will be smoother.

3. While the batter is having a rest, zest, pith, and segment the oranges (see Methods and Techniques, page 7). Add the 2 tablespoons (25 mL) of vodka. Let the orange segments soak it up.

4. If you have a crêpe pan, excellent! If not, improvise: use a non-stick frying pan. Lightly spray or grease the pan. I use a vegetable spray that hasn't any fluoro-carbons in it.

5. Heat the pan. While it's heating, gently stir the batter. Add approximately ⅓ cup (75 mL) of the batter to the pan. Tilt the pan so the batter covers the bottom. It's all in the wrist.

6. Cook until golden brown. Flip. Cook the other side.

7. Stack the crêpes between layers of parchment paper. It prevents them from sticking. No parchment paper? Wax paper works—not as well, but it does.

8. Cook all the crêpes (8 to 12). Store them wrapped in the fridge until the sauce is ready.

Showtime!

1. In a large frying pan, melt the butter. Add the marmalade, sugar, and lemon juice. Bring to a boil. You need to boil this for at least 2 to 3 minutes. It needs to thicken up before you add the next ingredient. Think molten steel as a visual.

2. After 2 to 3 minutes of boiling, stir in the orange juice.

3. Get the crêpes out of the fridge. Fold into quarters and swirl them into the sauce. Heat until simmering.

4. Add the ¼ cup (50 mL) of vodka. Bring to a boil. Turn off the heat and ignite, using a long-handled match. (Don't use a butane lighter of any kind—safety first.)

5. When the flames go out, add the vodka-soaked oranges and serve.

Cake

Marie Antoinette may have needed a major attitude adjustment, but she really was on to something when she said, "Let them eat cake." I'm with Madame Marie!

Cake Rules

1. Use ingredients at room temperature.

2. Use parchment paper to line cake pans. If you don't have any, dust the lightly greased pan with flour (or cocoa when baking chocolate cake).

3. Bake the cake on the middle rack.

4. Test for doneness with the old tooth-pick test: if it comes out clean, it's done.

5. Let the cake sit in the pan on a cooling rack for 10 minutes before taking it out of the pan. This 10-minute "time out" will help the cake to slide out of the pan effortlessly.

6. Cool on a cooling rack until the cake is at room temperature. Then apply icing.

Chocolate Fudge Cake with Mairlyn's "World-Famous" Fudge Icing

Makes one 8-inch (1.2 L), round layer cake; serve 10–16

I feel as though most of my life has been dedicated to creating the best chocolate cake. Now that may sound pathetic to a brain surgeon, but to a chocolate lover—we're talking a Nobel Prize in biochemistry.

When I was testing cake recipes, I tried every possible type—sponge, traditional, quick. I experimented with melted chocolate and cocoa powder. I compared butter, shortening, and margarine. I did it all. My neighbour Evelyne loved me. Every couple of days I'd send her the latest experiment. Through many trials, I did eventually reach my life's goal. But the one that won the blind taste test was a surprise. It doesn't have any butter or melted chocolate! It's a shortened cake with cocoa! Who knew?

It was also the quickest, easiest cake I made. Give it a try. You'll love it.

* Dutch cocoa powder has been processed. It's less bitter and darker in colour than regular cocoa powder. If you can't find Dutch cocoa, regular is fine.

1⅔ cups	all-purpose flour	400 mL
1½ cups	white sugar	375 mL
⅔ cup	Dutch cocoa powder*	150 mL
1½ tsp	baking soda	7 mL
1/2 cup	shortening, at room temperature	125 mL
1 cup	water	250 mL
½ cup	2% or skim milk	125 mL
2 tsp	lemon juice	10 mL
2	large eggs	2
1 tbsp	vanilla	15 mL

1. Preheat oven to 350°F (180°C). Grease two 8-inch (1.2 L) round pans. Dust bottoms with cocoa powder. (There's a joke waiting to happen.)

2. In a large mixing bowl, dump in the flour, sugar, cocoa, baking soda, and shortening.

3. In a smaller bowl, mix together the water, milk, lemon juice, eggs, and vanilla.

4. Dump—okay—*pour* this mixture into the flour mixture.

5. Using an electric mixer, mix on low speed for 30 seconds. Scrape the bowl to make sure all the ingredients are mixed in.

6. Turn power to medium. Mix for 2 minutes and 30 seconds, scraping the bowl once in a while. (What does *once in a while* really mean? Three times.)

7. Pour into prepared pans. Even out the batter.

8. Bake for 25 to 30 minutes or until a toothpick inserted comes out clean.

9. Cool in the pan on a cooling rack for 10 minutes.

10. Flip onto the cooling rack. Let cool completely.

11. Ice with my "World-Famous" Fudge Icing.

Mairlyn's "World-Famous" Fudge Icing

Enough to ice one 8-inch (1.2 L) layer cake with extras for licking

8 oz	semi-sweet chocolate	225 g
½ cup	Dutch cocoa powder*	125 mL
¾ cup	water	175 mL
½ cup	unsalted butter	125 mL
3 cups	icing sugar	750 mL

1. In a pot, over low heat, combine the chocolate, cocoa, water, and butter; stir constantly to prevent the dreaded chocolate-scorching. When just melted, remove from heat.

2. Stir in the icing sugar. (No, you're right, it doesn't look like icing, and no, I haven't lost my mind.)

3. Pour this chocolate liquid into a bowl and refrigerate until thick, 3 to 4 hours.

4. When thick, beat for 1 to 3 minutes or until creamy.

5. Frost cake. Lick bowl while standing over the sink. Make sure you wash your face before going out.

> * Dutch cocoa powder has been processed. It's less bitter and darker in colour than regular cocoa powder. If you can't find Dutch cocoa, regular is fine.

Chocolate Orange Cake

Makes one 8-inch (2.0 L), round layer cake or one 9 by 13-inch (3.5 L) flat cake; serves 10–16

A fudgy chocolate cake with just a hint of orange and no milk. I created it for my son, who can't have dairy products. Its light texture goes well with a chocolate glaze made with cocoa powder and icing sugar. I've also used this recipe for his birthday cake every year. It's been a train, a racing car, Batman, and the Taz—the Tasmanian devil!

1⅔ cups	all-purpose flour	400 mL
1½ cups	white sugar	375 mL
⅔ cup	cocoa powder	150 mL
1½ tsp	baking soda	7 mL
1 cup	orange juice	250 mL
½ cup	water	125 mL
2	large eggs	2
1 tsp	vanilla	5 mL
½ cup	shortening, at room temperature	125 mL

1. Preheat the oven to 350°F (180°C). Grease two 8-inch (2.0 L) round cake pans or one 9 x 13-inch (3.5 L) pan. Dust with cocoa powder.

2. In a large mixing bowl, mix together the flour, sugar, cocoa, and baking soda.

3. In a smaller bowl, measure out the orange juice, water, eggs, and vanilla.

4. Dump all of step 3 into the large mixing bowl. Add the shortening.

5. Using an electric mixer, mix on low speed for 30 seconds.

6. Turn power to medium. Mix for 2 minutes and 30 seconds, scraping the bowl three times.

7. Pour into prepared pans. Even out the batter.

8. Bake for 25 to 30 minutes for the two 8-inch (2.0 L) round pans and bake 30 minutes for the 9 x 13-inch (3.5 L) pan, or until a toothpick inserted comes out clean.

9. Cool in the pan on a cooling rack for 10 minutes.

10. Gently flip onto a cooling rack. Let cool completely.

11. Ice with your favourite icing or try my "World-Famous" Fudge Icing (page 173).

Chocolate Banana Cake

Makes one 8-inch (2.0 L), round three-layer cake; serves 10–16

Once again, a simple chocolate cake. This one is packed full of bananas. It's a one-bowl baby and pretty much foolproof. My son knows how to make this cake. Put everything into one bowl and mix. It doesn't get much easier than that.

1⅓ cups	all-purpose flour	325 mL
1 cup	whole wheat flour	250 mL
1¼ cups	white sugar	300 mL
3 tbsp	cocoa powder	45 mL
1½ cups	mashed very ripe bananas (see note #1 below)	375 mL
⅔ cup	sour milk (see note #2 below)	150 mL
⅔ cup	shortening, at room temperature	150 mL
3	large eggs	3
1¼ tsp	baking powder	6 mL
1¼ tsp	baking soda	6 mL
1 tsp	vanilla	5 mL

1. Preheat the oven to 350°F (180°C). Lightly grease three 8-inch (2.0 L) round cake pans. Line bottoms with parchment paper.

2. Dump all ingredients into a large mixing bowl in the order I've listed them.

3. Using an electric mixer on low, blend all the ingredients for 30 seconds, scraping the bowl often.

4. Turn power up to medium and continue mixing for 2 minutes and 30 seconds.

5. Pour the batter in equal amounts between the three pans. Even out the batter.

6. Bake for 35 to 40 minutes or until a toothpick inserted comes out clean.

7. Cool in the pan on a cooling rack for 10 minutes.

8. Gently flip onto a cooling rack. Let cool completely.

9. Ice with your favourite icing or use my "World-Famous" Fudge Icing (page 173).

Note #1 *Really ripe bananas: They are those ugly-looking, black ones most people throw away.* **Don't**—*they are loaded with flavour. Freeze them whole in their peel. When you need one, thaw Mr. Banana on a plate, cut off the end, and squeeze out the thawed, very ripe, mushy banana. Looks gross; tastes great.*
Note #2 *Sour milk: Don't have any rotten milk in your fridge? You must have teenagers in your house. Well, you can sour up some good milk by adding 1 tablespoon (15 mL) of lemon juice, lime juice, or vinegar.*

Lick the Spoon!

Poppy Seed Cake with Zesty Lemon Icing

Makes one 9-inch (1.5 L), round layer cake; serves 10–16

One of my oldest and dearest friends has a cottage in Muskoka. Every summer, Michale and I make meals for anywhere from 8 to 18 people. We call ourselves the "M&M Cooking Show" because the assorted guests stand on the cottage's massive deck and watch us cook through the kitchen window. We think we're hilarious. We aren't, but cooking a gourmet dinner for 18 in a kitchen the size of a small woodshed *can* be funny, especially with enough white wine.

This is one of Michale's recipes. She has never measured anything in her entire life—which drives me insane—so it took several attempts to get this recipe down on paper.

Cake

¾ cup	poppy seeds	175 mL
1 cup	skim milk	250 mL
⅔ cup	unsalted butter	150 mL
1½ cups	white sugar	375 mL
4	large eggs, separated	4
2 cups	cake and pastry flour	500 mL
2½ tsp	baking powder	12 mL

1. Preheat the oven to 350°F (180°C). Lightly grease two 9-inch (1.5 L) round pans. Line the bottom of the pans with parchment paper.

2. Mix the poppy seeds and the milk together. Let sit.

3. In a large bowl, cream the butter. Gradually beat in the sugar until light and fluffy.

4. Beat in the yolks, one at a time.

5. On a sheet of wax paper, sift together the flour and baking powder.

6. Add the flour mixture and the milk mixture to the butter mixture in this order, gently mixing after each addition: half of the flour mixture, all of the milk mixture, and the remaining flour mixture.

7. Beat the egg whites until stiff—remember to use a clean, non-plastic bowl.

8. Fold the whites into the batter; pour the batter into the prepared pans.

9. Bake for 20 to 30 minutes or until a toothpick inserted comes out clean.

10. Cool in the pan on a cooling rack for 10 minutes.

11. Flip onto the cooling rack; let cool completely.

12. Ice with your favourite icing or try my Zesty Lemon Icing.

Zesty Lemon Icing

½ cup	unsalted butter	125 mL
2⅓ cups	icing sugar	575 mL
5 tbsp	lemon juice	75 mL
	Zest of 1 lemon	

1. With a hand beater, blend the butter, icing sugar, lemon juice, and zest until smooth. Ice cake.

Hazelnut Sponge Cake with Chocolate Brandy Glaze

Makes one 9-inch (2.5 L) cake; serves 8–10

When I entertain, I like to do as much as I can the day before—phone the caterer, book a massage and manicure. I wish! No, the day before, I grocery shop, buy my flowers, clean only the rooms my company has to see, and do as much of the cooking as I can.

This preparation usually includes washing the greens, making the soup, setting the table, arranging the flowers, and whenever possible, making the dessert.

This cake is a perfect fit for my entertaining criteria. It's quick, easy, and elegant, and it tastes better the day after you make it.

6	large eggs, separated	6
¾ cup	white sugar	175 mL
6 tbsp	orange brandy	90 mL
2½ cups	toasted and ground hazelnuts*	625 mL
½ cup	all-purpose flour	125 mL

1. Preheat the oven to 350°F (180°C). Line the bottom of a 9-inch (2.5 L) springform pan with parchment paper.

2. In a medium-sized bowl, beat the yolks for 2 minutes at high speed. Add the sugar, 1 tablespoon (15 mL) at a time. This step should take 12 to 14 minutes. So use a Mixmaster or read a book while you hold your electric hand mixer.

3. Beat in the brandy. Lick measuring cup.

4. Clean off the beaters in hot soapy water. Dry. In a non-plastic bowl, beat the egg whites until stiff.

5. Mix the ground hazelnuts and flour together.

6. Fold them into the brandy mixture.

7. Fold in the whites. Think gentle. Pour into the prepared pan. Even out the batter.

8. Bake for 40 to 45 minutes or until a toothpick inserted comes out clean.

9. Cool in a pan on a cooling rack for 10 minutes.

10. Using a sharp knife, cut between the edge of the cake and the pan. Unlock the spring and gently remove the sides. Peel off the paper.

11. Continue cooling until it's at room temperature.

12. Set on serving dish or cake stand. Glaze with Chocolate Brandy Glaze.

> **Note** *Cover the cake to prevent it from drying out overnight.*

Chocolate Brandy Glaze

¾ cup	semi-sweet chocolate chips	175 mL
2 tbsp	butter	25 mL
1 tbsp	orange brandy	15 mL
2 tbsp	hot water	25 mL

1. In a small, heavy saucepan over low heat, stir together the chocolate chips, butter, brandy, and hot water. When just melted, remove from heat.

2. Let cool for 1 to 2 minutes. Pour it over the cake, letting it drip down the sides.

3. Serve—tomorrow? Yes, it actually will taste better tomorrow. Console yourself by licking the chocolate glaze out of the pot.

> *To toast hazelnuts, use a heavy frying pan. Turn the heat up to medium-high. Add the whole hazelnuts. Stir often. Keep a close watch or they'll burn. When the skins start peeling off, take the pan off the heat. This whole process takes about 5 minutes. Put the hot nuts on a clean tea towel and roll them around. This will skin them. Remove the nuts and throw out the skins. Grind the nuts in a food processor. Or buy more expensive, less fresh, already ground hazelnuts. Take your pick.*

Carrot Cake with Amazing Cream Cheese Icing

Makes one 8-inch (1.2 L), round layer cake; serves 12–16

I've been making this carrot cake recipe since the seventies, when I dreamed of becoming a hippie. I was only 16 at the time and my conservative parents said "no." Being the ever-obedient daughter, I just dressed like one instead.

I felt like Mother Earth in my flowing skirts, preaching the healthy aspects of whole wheat flour, wheat germ, honey, and oil.

Well, some things are ageless, and speaking of aging (ba-da-boom), bake this the day before, then ice it, and refrigerate overnight. Aging mellows the cake. Funny, aging hasn't done the same thing for me.

1¼ cups	whole wheat flour	300 mL
⅓ cup	wheat germ	75 mL
¼ cup	bran	50 mL
1¾ tsp	baking soda	9 mL
1½ tsp	baking powder	7 mL
1 tbsp	cinnamon	15 mL
¼ tsp	ground nutmeg	1 mL
Pinch	ground cloves	Pinch
1 cup	toasted and ground hazelnuts (see page 179)	250 mL
2½ cups	grated carrots	625 mL
½ cup	currants (optional)	125 mL
2	large eggs	2
1 cup	canola oil	250 mL
1 cup	liquid honey	250 mL

1. Preheat oven to 300°F (150°C). Lightly grease two 8-inch (1.2 L) round pans. Line bottoms with parchment paper.

2. Mix together in a large bowl the flour, wheat germ, bran, baking soda, baking powder, cinnamon, nutmeg, and cloves.

3. Add the ground nuts that you painstakingly slaved over. Toss.

4. Add the carrots and currants, if using, and toss until everything is coated. We'll call this the dry ingredients.

5. Beat together the eggs, oil, and honey. Now pour into the dry ingredients.

6. Mix until well combined.

7. Spread evenly in the prepared pans.

8. Bake for 40 to 45 minutes or until a toothpick inserted comes out clean.

9. Cool for 10 minutes in the pans on a cooling rack. Gently remove cakes from the pans. Continue cooling on the rack until totally cool.

10. Ice with Amazing Cream Cheese Icing (below).

Amazing Cream Cheese Icing

⅓ cup	unsalted butter	75 mL
8 oz	cream cheese	250 g
3 cups	icing sugar	750 mL

1. Blend the butter, cream cheese, and icing sugar until creamy. Ice the cake.

2. Garnish with chopped hazelnuts. I put fresh nasturtiums from my garden on the top when they are in season. They look sharp!

Carrot Cake Rules

1. When measuring the carrots, don't pack them into the measuring cup or the cake will be soggy.

2. Don't use raisins. They will make the cake fall apart.

3. Measure the oil first; then measure the honey in the same measuring cup. The honey will just slide out.

4. This is a gentle cake, so be very careful when you remove it from the pan and when you ice it.

5. Store the cake in the fridge.

range Sponge Cake with Marmalade Glaze

Makes one 9-inch (3.0 L) tubular cake; serves 8–10

My grandmother made a great sponge cake. Not being able to leave well enough alone, I began a long quest to improve upon it. Attempting to improve or fix something—like a broken toilet, a flat tire, or a bad spouse—is well worth the effort. Well, surprise, surprise, I had to change only one thing to make Gran's cake even better. (Too bad changing one thing couldn't fix those other little problems.)

4	large eggs, separated	4
2 tbsp	frozen orange juice concentrate, thawed	25 mL
12 tbsp	white sugar	180 mL
½ tsp	vanilla	2 mL
½ tsp	cream of tartar	2 mL
¾ cup	all-purpose flour	175 mL

1. Preheat oven to 325°F (160°C). Find your 9-inch (3 L) angel-food tube pan.

2. Beat the yolks with the orange juice concentrate for 2 minutes.

3. Add 6 tablespoons (90 mL) of sugar and beat for 5 minutes or until thick and creamy. Beat in vanilla. (Hope you have a Mixmaster.)

4. Now beat the whites. Use clean beaters and a medium-sized glass or non-plastic bowl. Beat the whites until foamy. Add the cream of tartar; beat until frothy.

5. Add the remaining 6 tablespoons (90 mL) of sugar, 1 tablespoon (15 mL) at a time, beating until the whites reach the stiff-peak stage. (Home-economist-speak for "when you pick the beaters up, a lovely, stiff, keep-your-shape mountain peak appears.")

6. Gently fold the beaten yolks into the beaten whites.

7. Fold in the flour even more gently.

8. Spoon the batter into the angel food pan. Even out.

9. Bake for 30 to 35 minutes or until the top looks dry.

10. Cool upside down. Remove from pan. Glaze with Marmalade Glaze.

> **Note** This is a great family cake, or as my friend Marianne says, "You can serve it to the kids without worrying they'll have a big chocolate rush." Parent-approved for kids.

Marmalade Glaze

2 tbsp	unsalted butter	25 mL
2 tbsp	white sugar	25 mL
½ cup	marmalade	125 mL
1 tbsp	frozen orange juice concentrate	15 mL

1. In a saucepan, melt the butter. Add the sugar, marmalade, and orange juice concentrate. Stir constantly until it starts to boil. Let boil for 1 minute; remove from heat.

2. Let cool for 5 minutes. Pour over cooled cake and serve.

Pie

Mair's Favourite Pastry

I have tried every conceivable pastry recipe. I've used pastry blenders, food processors, two knives—I've even melted the fat. Speaking of which, I've tried butter, shortening, lard, and oil.

Of all I've tried, the best is the pastry recipe printed on a box of lard! It is foolproof. My klutzy, wonderful sister even attempted a sabotage—to no avail.

Please don't send me any letters on the evils of lard: we are talking *pastry*. The main ingredient *is* fat. Don't waste your time trying to make healthy pastry— that's an oxymoron. Make it with lard and just have a tiny piece of pie.

So, with my humble apologies to Julia Child and Betty Crocker, here's my favourite: the Tenderflake recipe.

6 cups	cake and pastry flour OR 5½ cups (1.4 L) all-purpose flour	1.5 L
2 tsp	salt	10 mL
1 lb	Tenderflake lard	454 g
1 tbsp	vinegar	15 mL
1	large egg, slightly beaten Water	1

1. Mix together the flour and salt.

2. Cut in the Tenderflake with a pastry blender or with two knives until mixture resembles coarse oatmeal.

3. In a 1-cup (250 mL) measure, combine the vinegar and egg. Add water to make 1 cup (250 mL). Gradually stir liquid into Tenderflake mixture. Add only enough liquid to make dough cling together.

4. Gather dough into a ball and divide into six portions. If desired, wrap unused portions and refrigerate or freeze.

5. Roll out each portion on a lightly floured surface. If dough is sticking, chill for 1 to 2 hours.

6. Transfer dough to a 9-inch (23 cm) pie plate. Trim and flute the edge and bake according to your pie recipe.

pple Pie

Makes one 8-inch (20 cm) pie

An apple pie is only as good as the apples you choose. I like combining the great, all-purpose McIntosh with the tart crisp northern spy. It gives a great texture to the pie. If you can't find northern spy, use a Granny Smith.

	Pastry for two 8-inch (20 cm) pie shells	
2	McIntosh apples, peeled, cored, and sliced	2
4	northern spy OR Granny Smith apples, peeled, cored and sliced	4
1 tbsp	lemon juice	15 mL
1 cup	brown sugar	250 mL
1½ tsp	cinnamon	7 mL
Pinch	freshly grated nutmeg	Pinch
3 tbsp	all-purpose flour	45 mL
1 tbsp	unsalted butter	15 mL
	White sugar	

1. Preheat oven to 425°F (220°C).

2. Roll pastry out so that it is about 2 inches (5 cm) bigger than the pie plate.

3. Gently transfer to pie plate.

4. In a large bowl, mix together the apples, lemon juice, brown sugar, cinnamon, nutmeg, and flour.

5. Pour into pie shell; dot with the butter.

6. Roll out the top piece of pastry. Gently transfer to pie.

7. Fold and roll top edge over the bottom edge. Press to seal; flute.

8. Prick holes in the top and sprinkle with a little sugar. Loosely cover with foil.

9. Bake for 15 minutes at 425°F (220°C).

10. Reduce heat to 350°F (180°C) and continue baking for 30 minutes.

11. Remove foil and continue baking for 20 minutes. Cool and serve.

Apple Cranberry Pie

Makes one 9-inch (23 cm) pie

I was doing some home-economist work on a cookbook several years ago. My job was to follow the recipes to a tee; I was the triple tester.

One of the recipes called for cranberries. Well, it was June and cranberries weren't in season. I couldn't even find frozen cranberries.

I phoned the head home economist on the project to tell her my problem and to see if she had any cranberries. I'll never forget her reply, "Well, Mairlyn, a good home economist always has cranberries in her freezer."

My first thought was to tell her where she should keep hers, but my better judgement got in the way. I humbly agreed with her and to this day I keep cranberries, raspberries, strawberries, and blueberries in my freezer. I'm living for the day she calls to see if I have any.

	Pastry for two 9-inch (23 cm) pie shells	
4	large McIntosh apples, peeled, cored, and sliced	4
1 cup	cranberries, frozen or fresh	250 mL
¾ cup	white sugar	175 mL
⅓ cup	brown sugar	75 mL
1 tbsp	cinnamon	15 mL
	zest of 1 orange	
2 tbsp	orange juice	25 mL
2 tbsp	all-purpose flour	25 mL
1 tbsp	unsalted butter	15 mL
	white sugar	
1	large egg, beaten (optional)	1

1. Preheat oven to 425°F (220°C).

2. Roll out pastry so that it is about 2 inches (5 cm) bigger than the pie plate.

3. Gently transfer to pie plate.

4. In a large bowl, mix together the apples, cranberries, white sugar, brown sugar, cinnamon, orange zest, orange juice, and flour.

5. Pour into pie shell. Dot with butter.

6. Roll out the top piece of pastry. Gently transfer to pie.

7. Fold and roll top edge over the bottom edge. Press to seal; flute.

8. Prick holes in the top and sprinkle with sugar. Or brush with 1 beaten egg and then sprinkle with sugar. This latter variation will turn the crust a golden brown. Loosely cover with foil.

9. Bake for 20 minutes.

10. Reduce heat to 350°F (180°C) and bake for 20 minutes; remove foil.

11. Bake for 20 minutes more. Cool and serve.

Rhubarb Pie

Makes one 9-inch (23 cm) pie

A not-too-sweet version of a spring classic.

	Pastry for two 9-inch (23 cm) pie shells	
5–6 cups	chopped rhubarb	1.25–1.5 L
1 cup	white sugar	250 mL
1 cup	brown sugar	250 mL
1 tbsp	cinnamon	15 mL
½ cup	all-purpose flour	125 mL
1 tbsp	unsalted butter	15 mL
	White sugar	

1. Preheat oven to 425°F (220°C).

2. Roll out pastry so that it is about 2 inches (5 cm) bigger than the pie plate.

3. Gently transfer to pie plate.

4. In a large bowl, mix together the rhubarb, white sugar, brown sugar, cinnamon, and flour.

5. Pour into pie shell; dot with butter.

6. Roll out the top piece of pastry; gently transfer to pie.

7. Fold and roll top edge over the bottom edge. Press to seal; flute.

8. Prick holes in the top and sprinkle with a little sugar. Loosely cover with foil.

9. Bake for 30 minutes. Remove foil.

10. Reduce heat to 350°F (180°C) and bake for 30 more minutes. Cool and serve.

each Pie

Makes one 9-inch (23 cm) pie

Peach pie is summer to me—so is cellulite, but I digress. Its golden colours served on a chilled plate (I'm talking about the peaches now) with a scoop of French vanilla ice cream will give you cellulite. But I've gotten to an age where I don't actually care any more. Bring on the pie.

	Pastry for two 9-inch (23 cm) pie shells	
4 cups	sliced peaches	1 L
2 tsp	lemon juice	10 mL
⅔ cup	white sugar	150 mL
3 tbsp	all-purpose flour	45 mL
½ tsp	cinnamon	2 mL
	Zest of 1 lemon	
1 tbsp	unsalted butter	15 mL

1. Preheat oven to 425°F (220°C).

2. Roll out pastry so that it is about 2 inches (5 cm) bigger than the pie plate.

3. Gently transfer to pie plate.

4. In a large bowl, mix together the peaches, lemon juice, sugar, flour, cinnamon, and lemon zest.

5. Pour into pastry shell. Dot with butter.

6. Roll out the top piece of pastry. Gently transfer to pie.

7. Fold and roll top edge over the bottom edge. Press to seal; flute.

8. Prick holes in the top. Sprinkle with a little sugar. Loosely cover with foil.

9. Bake for 35 minutes. Remove foil.

10. Reduce heat to 400°F (200°C). Bake for 10 minutes more. Cool and serve.

Note *While pie is baking, do aerobics for 1 hour to pre-burn off the 465 calories you'll eat up with one slice of pie.*

Lick the Spoon!

Cheesecake

Cheesecake was first mentioned in literature as a dessert in 1440. I feel that only something really amazing could last that many centuries.

Here is my tribute to luscious, creamy, throw-out-your-bathroom-scale cheesecake.

arbled Cheesecake

Serves 10–12

Every so often, I hit it lucky. I win $10 in the lottery, my car doesn't break down in a month with an r in it, or I create a recipe that turns out great the first time.

This cheesecake comes from one of my lucky moments. I calculated the ratio of cream cheese to sugar to eggs in my favourite cheesecake recipes and came up with this combination, baked it, and— boy! Even I was impressed. I think all that science and math I took at the University of British Columbia finally paid off. Here's a practical application of ratios.

Cheesecake

1 lb	light cream cheese, at room temperature	500 g
¾ cup	white sugar	175 mL
1 tsp	vanilla	5 mL
1 cup	light sour cream	250 mL
3	large eggs, at room temperature	3
4 oz	semi-sweet chocolate	113 g

Crust

2½ cups	chocolate cookie crumbs	625 mL
¼ cup	butter, melted	50 mL

1. Preheat oven to 350°F (180°C). Line the bottom of an 8-inch (2 L) springform pan with parchment paper.

2. *Gently* beat the cream cheese. Over-beating will contribute to a cracked top.

3. Beat in the sugar and vanilla until smooth.

4. Beat in the sour cream.

5. Beat in the eggs, one at a time, until smooth.

6. Melt the chocolate.

7. Remove ¾ cup (175 mL) of the cream cheese mixture and add to the melted chocolate, stirring until well combined. Set aside. Let the fillings rest while you prepare the crust.

8. Mix together the cookie crumbs and butter until well combined.

9. Press into the springform pan. Bake for 10 minutes.

10. Pour in the plain cream cheese filling.

11. Spoon the chocolate mixture over top. With a knife, swirl the chocolate mixture into the plain filling to create a marbled effect.

12. Bake for 1 hour. Turn the oven off and open the door slightly. Cool for 1 hour in the oven.

13. Refrigerate for 1 hour. Remove from pan. Keep refrigerated until serving time.

Pumpkin Cheesecake

Menu writing is an art form in itself. Here's how I'd write up this pumpkin cheesecake: "Luscious, creamy pumpkin cheesecake abounding with autumn's favourite flavours—cinnamon, nutmeg, and fresh ginger—on a cookie-crumb base made with crispy gingersnaps." Feel like ordering it? Well you'll have to make it first.

Cheesecake

24 oz	light cream cheese, at room temperature	750 g
¾ cup	brown sugar	175 mL
4	large eggs, room temperature	4
2 cups	canned pumpkin purée	500 mL
½ cup	evaporated skim milk	125 mL
¼ cup	cornstarch	50 mL
1 tbsp	cinnamon	15 mL
2 tsp	grated fresh ginger	10 mL
¼ tsp	ground nutmeg	1 mL

Crust

2½ cups	gingersnap cookie crumbs (36–40 cookies)	625 mL
½ cup	unsalted butter, melted	125 mL

1. Preheat oven to 325°F (160°C). Line the bottom of a 9-inch (2.5 L) springform pan with parchment paper.

2. In a bowl, gently beat the cream cheese. (Overbeating will contribute to a cracked top, which looks bad. Tastes the same, just looks bad.)

3. Beat in the brown sugar until smooth.

4. Beat in the eggs, one at a time.

5. Stir in the pumpkin, evaporated skim milk, cornstarch, cinnamon, ginger, and nutmeg. Set aside.

6. Put the cookies in the food processor or blender and grind into fine crumbs.

7. Mix together the cookie crumbs and butter until well combined.

8. Press into the springform pan. Bake for 10 minutes.

9. Pour cream cheese filling onto crust.

10. Bake for 1 hour and then turn off the oven. Keep the oven door closed. Leave the cheesecake in the oven for 30 minutes.

11. Open the oven door slightly and let the cheesecake cool for 3 hours.

12. Remove from the springform pan and refrigerate several hours or overnight.

13. Serve with whipped cream and grated chocolate, if desired.

hocolate Caramel Pecan Cheesecake

Serves 12–20!

At first glance you're thinking, "Wow, there are lots of steps and ingredients— I'm never making this. I don't care if Mrs. Clinton served this to the Queen, I'm not even going to try."

Well, don't let a whole lot of steps and a couple of ingredients scare you off.

This decadent cheesecake tastes like a giant Turtle, and I don't mean a marine tortoise. It has all the right ingredients— pecans, caramel, and chocolate. So get out your "fat pants" and indulge.

P.S. You don't want to know how many grams of fat this baby packs in one slice. After one taste, you won't care.

Caramel Sauce

¾ cup + 2 tbsp	brown sugar	175 mL + 25 mL
½ cup	whipping cream	125 mL
½ cup	corn syrup	125 mL
¼ cup	unsalted butter	50 mL
1 tsp	vanilla	5 mL

There are two ways to make the caramel sauce: Way #1, without a candy thermometer, and Way #2, with a candy thermometer.

Way #1

In a heavy saucepan over medium heat, mix together the brown sugar, whipping cream, corn syrup, and butter. Stir constantly. Bring to a boil. Stop stirring and adjust the heat so the caramel will not boil over. (If you've ever been to Yellowstone National Park and seen the boiling lava, this is what the caramel should look like. For everyone else, just think of boiling lava. You'll be fine.) Let it boil like this for 5 minutes. Remove it from the heat and stir once. Let it cool for 3 minutes and add the vanilla. It will boil up again. Don't lick the spoon! Pour it into a heat-tempered glass measuring cup. This recipe makes 1½ cups (375 mL). Let it cool for 3 hours at room temperature.

Way #2

In a heavy saucepan over medium heat, mix together the brown sugar, whipping cream, corn syrup, and butter. Stir constantly. Bring to a boil. Let it reach 231°F (111°C) on the candy thermometer or bring to the soft ball stage. When either the temperature or the candy stage has been reached, remove from heat. Stir once. Let it cool for 3 minutes and add the vanilla. It will boil up again. Don't lick the spoon! Remember, 3 minutes ago it was 231°F (111°C)—yikes! Pour it into a heat-tempered glass measuring cup. This recipe makes 1½ cups (375 mL). Let it cool for 3 hours at room temperature.

While the caramel is cooling, make the cheesecake.

Cheesecake

1 lb	cream cheese, at room temperature	500 g
½ cup	white sugar	125 mL
2 tsp	vanilla	10 mL
2	large eggs, at room temperature	2

Crust

2¼ cups	chocolate cookie crumbs	550 mL
½ cup	unsalted butter, melted	125 mL
1 cup	whole pecans	250 mL

Glaze

1½ cups	semi-sweet chocolate chips	375 mL
3 tbsp	hot water	45 mL
3 tbsp	unsalted butter	45 mL

1. Preheat oven to 350°F (180°C). Line the bottom of a 9-inch (2.5 L) springform pan with parchment paper.

2. *Gently* beat the cream cheese. Overbeating will contribute to a cracked top.

3. Beat in the sugar and vanilla until well combined.

4. Beat in the eggs, one at a time. Let sit while you make the crust.

5. Mix together the cookie crumbs and butter until well combined.

6. Press into the springform pan.

7. In a baking dish sprinkle the pecans

8. Put both the pecans and the crust in the oven for 10 minutes.

9. Ding—10 minutes is up, remove from the oven. Set the pecans aside.

10. Pour the cheesecake mixture on top of the cookie-crumb crust.

11. Even out and bake for 35 to 40 minutes. Turn the oven off and leave the oven door slightly ajar. Cool in the oven for 40 minutes. This helps prevent surface cracking.

12. Remove to a cooling rack. Run a knife around the edge. Let cool to room temperature. Remove the sides and bottom of the springform pan. Put the cheesecake on a serving dish.

13. Pour on the caramel sauce. Spread out evenly but not quite to the edge. Lay on the cooled, toasted pecans. Refrigerate for 1 hour.

14. Put the chocolate chips, hot water, and butter in a saucepan. Melt mixture over low heat, stirring constantly.

15. Pour the chocolate mixture over the cheesecake. Let it drip over the sides.

16. And finally, there you have it: A Giant Turtle Cheesecake. Refrigerate overnight. Let "warm" up for 20 minutes before cutting. It needs this warming-up time so the flavours will really come through. If it's too cold, you won't get all the nuances!

Pitfall *You just read the "refrigerate overnight" part, and you wanted to serve this for supper tonight. Don't panic. As long as you chill it for at least 2 hours, it will be okay. It just tastes better the next day. Remember for next time and, believe me, you'll make this a lot.*

Menu Planning

or What to Serve When

ary Tyler Moore, on her TV show, always had terrible parties. She'd plan and plan, and something awful would happen. She'd run out of food, the guest of honour wouldn't show, or the power would go off.

Years ago I became famous for "Mary" parties. I'd invite sixty people, six would show, and I'd have a fire in the oven.

I finally figured it out—*too many plans, too many people*. So now I'm famous for smart little dinner parties. I can handle a sit-down for eight or a stand-up for thirty. Here's my rule: the bigger the crowd, the simpler the menu.

So now the fun part starts: planning a dinner party. You've read the book and you've picked out the recipes you are going to try. But what goes with what, and what do you serve when? Here are some ideas.

Your boss and her husband are coming to dinner.
- Asparagus with Lime Mayonnaise
- Mixed Baby Greens with Mango Chutney Dressing
- Chicken Breasts with Tarragon and Mustard
- Mashed Potatoes
- Swiss Chard or broccoli
- Orange and Scented Geranium Sorbet
- fresh strawberries

You're making a cozy winter supper for just the two of you. Candlelight please.
- Romaine with Avocado Dressing
- French Onion Soup
- crusty bread
- No dessert will be necessary.

You have to supply a meal at the cottage.
- Caesar Salad
- Mairlyn's Spicy, Blow-Your-Head-Off Pasta
- My Favourite Chocolate Chip Cookies
- fresh fruit

It's Valentine's Day
- Make reservations.

You have a terrible cold.
- Baby Spinach with Spicy Vinaigrette
- Curried Chicken Soup
- Flaming Vodka Orange Crêpes—the orange juice may help.

Your best friend and her third husband are coming to dinner.
- Broccoli Soup
- Blackened Orange Roughy with Citrus Salsa
- Plain Couscous
- green beans
- Chocolate Banana Cake

You're making a lovely summer's dinner—just the two of you.
- Quickies
- Rotini with Feta and Tomatoes
- Peach Pie

It's Hockey Night in Canada—regular season.
- Curried Shrimp

It's Hockey Night in Canada—playoffs.
- Curried Shrimp—served buck naked.

Your friends are dropping by for a summer dinner.
- Potato Salad
- Salsa-Broiled Chicken Breasts
- corn
- Pea Salad
- fresh fruit and Family Brownies

Your partner's less-than-exciting friend Lloyd is coming to dinner.
- Mair's House Salad
- Family-Style Sole
- Rice with Green Onions and Peas
- Carrots
- Apple Pie

Your girlfriends are coming for an afternoon tea party.
- tea
- Scones with raspberry jam
- Lemon Bars
- Gingersnaps
- Chocolate Caramel Pecan Cheesecake

The third annual Chocolate Lovers Society business meeting is at your house.
- Better-Than-Sex Brownies
- My Favourite Chocolate Chip Cookies
- No-Bake Chocolate Treats
- Chocolate Caramel Pecan Cheesecake
- Tylenol

Your husband's ex-girlfriend and her new boyfriend are coming to dinner.
- Cheese Pâté
- Quick Black Bean Soup
- Vegetarian Chili
- Quick Dinner Bread
- Carrot Cake with Amazing Cream Cheese Icing
- (Be the only one who takes the anti-gas solution, Beano.)

Your good neighbours have high cholesterol. You promised to cook low-fat.

- Greens and Grapefruit
- Poached Sole with Citrus and Fresh Ginger
- Dad's Rice Pilaf
- Chocolate Banana Sorbet

Your sister and her husband are coming over for a casual supper.

- Caesar Salad
- Ratatouille
- crusty Italian bread
- Rhubarb Crisp

Friends from the drop-in centre and their kids are coming to dinner. Help! Hope they go home before the house gets wrecked.

- Shells with Italian Chili Sauce
- Carrots and broccoli
- Whoopie Cookies

Your parents are coming over—bring out the good china.

- Marinated Mushrooms
- Butternut Squash Soup
- Orange Roughy Wrapped in Phyllo with Mango Salsa
- Couscous Pilaf
- green beans
- Apple Cranberry Pie

Your daughter brings home her new vegetarian boyfriend (summer menu).

- Salsa and corn chips
- New Wave Spinach Salad
- Plain-and-Simple Plum Tomato Sauce on fresh fettucine
- crusty Italian bread
- Lemon Sorbet

Amazingly enough, she is still dating Mr. Vegetarian in January (winter menu).

- Greens and Grapefruit
- Spanish Beans and Rice
- steamed broccoli
- Apple Crisp (using the topping recipe from Rhubarb Crisp)
- Beano

Your husband's boss is coming over with his skinny little wife, Yasmine. You want to wow the socks off them but not be in the kitchen the whole night.

- Peppercorn Pâté
- Wild Mushroom Soup
- Cornish Hens with Cranberries and wild rice
- Hazelnut Sponge Cake with Chocolate Brandy Glaze
- liqueurs

Index